LUTHERAN
HIGH SCHOOL
RELIGION SERIES ®

I0088597

Which Way Is the Right Way?

A Study of Christianity, Cults and Other Religions

Student Book

By Bruce Frederickson

Edited by Board for Parish Services Staff
Editor: Arnold E. Schmidt

CONCORDIA

Publishing House
St. Louis

Editorial Secretary: Phoebe Wellman

Write to Library for the Blind, 1333 S. Kirkwood Road, St. Louis, MO 63122-7295 to obtain *Which Way Is the Right Way? A Study of Christianity, Cults, and Other Religions.* (Student Book) in braille or sightsaving print for the visually impaired.

Contents

To the Student

What will it be like to leave home—to be completely on your own for the first time, like when you go away to college, join the Armed Forces, or report to your first year-round, full-time job?

You can be sure you'll meet people very different from yourself. Their skin will be a different color or they'll wear different-style clothes and eat different kinds of foods. Maybe one of these people will be a roommate and you will date another one. Maybe they will talk with you about another difference—their religious beliefs.

How will you respond?

Will you know what they're talking about? Will you know enough about their beliefs to carry on a conversation with them? Will you be able to talk to them about your faith in Jesus—without "turning them off"?

Of course, you will need to trust God to guide you at that time. After Jesus warned His disciples that they would face persecution because of their faith, He promised them, **"Just say whatever is given you at the time, for it is not you speaking, but the Holy Spirit"** **(Mark 13:11).** As a child of God, you can rely on that promise.

God is preparing you *right now* for that day. One way He is preparing you is through this course on *Which Way Is the Right Way? A Study of Christianity, Cults, and Other Religions.* May He through this study keep you faithful to Him and equip you to witness effectively to people who do not know Jesus as their Savior.

The Editor

UNIT 1

Religion! What's That?

There are only two religions in the world: the religion of people (which says that we must *do* something to appease God's wrath), and the religion of God (which says that God, in Christ, has done everything for us). He sent His Son, Jesus Christ, to die on the cross for our sins. He brought us closer to Himself. In the words of Paul, **"God was reconciling the world to Himself in Christ, not counting men's sins against them" (2 Corinthians 5:19).** This is the message everyone needs to hear!

During this course you will learn many new things. You will also review some things you've known for a long time. The most important message for you is that God loves all people, just as He loves you. He wants you to know that, so that you can be motivated to share the great Good News with others.

By learning about other religions you'll be better able to witness your faith to them. You'll find ways in which religions are similar and ways in which they are different. You'll discover some things about other religions that will help you avoid saying something offensive to them. And you'll also discover situations in which God can particularly use you to His glory by sharing what Jesus means to you.

Before you share with people of other religions, be sure you know your own religion well. Above all, you need a firm personal relationship with Jesus Christ. Read His Word often and speak to Him in prayer frequently.

Notice the Bible verses at the end of each session. Mark them in your Bibles. Try to remember the connection between the verse and the point of the lesson. Then meditate on that verse as you go about your daily life. And when the Lord places before you an opportunity to share your faith, use His Word!

May the Lord give you great wisdom in your studying. May He give you a sense of joy in knowing Him personally. And may He empower you and make you a bold witness to His name!

Session 1

What Is a Religion?

While speaking to some Pharisees and teachers of the Law, Jesus quoted the Old Testament prophet Isaiah: **"These people honor Me with their lips, but their hearts are far from Me. They worship Me in vain; their teachings are but rules taught by men"** (Matthew 15:8–9). Jesus judged their religiosity. He told them it consisted only in empty rituals.

WHAT IS RELIGION?

1. Write your definition of *religion* on a separate sheet of paper. Then use *religion* in a sentence, but not in a "churchy" sense.

2. Share your definition or sentence with others. Did you learn anything further about the meaning of the word religion?

Now look up the word in a dictionary and compare its definition there with yours. What is the difference between using the word in a "churchy" sense and using it otherwise? How does this help your understanding of *religion*?

YES AND NO IN A TAXI CAB

Here is a conversation between a clergyman and a taxicab driver. The driver throws the first words over his shoulder in the direction of the clerical collar he glimpsed when the clergyman got into the cab.

Driver: Where to?

Clergyman: Airport, please.

Driver: You a priest or something?

Clergyman: I'm a Lutheran pastor.

Driver: That so? I used to go to a Lutheran church. St. Paul's on the north side. Pastor X baptized my kids. Know him?

Clergyman: Yes, I do.

Driver: Yeah? I liked him a lot, but I don't go much any more. (Pause.) You know, I got a theory about religion. All religions are OK if you practice them.

Clergyman (*not interested*): That so?

Driver: Yeah! Every religion is good so long as you put it into practice.

Clergyman (*suddenly deciding to take the conversation seriously*): Could I test your theory?

Driver: Sure, go ahead. Always like to talk about religion.

Clergyman: What would you say about Hitler and Nazism? Was that a good religion?

Driver (*surprised*): That wasn't no religion!

Clergyman: But it had many of the characteristics of a religion—rituals, doctrines, heretics. Most important, Hitler demanded and got total loyalty and unquestioning obedience. The institutions of Nazism replaced those of Christianity almost item by item. What does that do to your theory that every religion is good so long as you put it into practice?

Driver: Well you sure got a crazy definition of religion!

Clergyman: Let's look at another time people think of religion—when someone dies.

Driver: Yeah! I've thought about that. It bothers me when I think that one of my kids might die. I used to go into their rooms at night when they were little, and they'd be sleeping, and I'd love them so much I could just feel it. I knew if one of 'em died it would be awful. I knew I couldn't stand it. I would even pray once in a while that God won't let 'em die. I thought going to church might help. But then there didn't really seem to be a God. 'Scuse me, Reverend. I don't mean to insult you.

Clergyman: That's OK. Go ahead.

Driver: Finally it just seemed useless, all that singing and praying and sitting and standing. Mind you, I'm not against religion. Good for the kids to get some starch into their lives, something to keep 'em straight.

But I knew that if something was going to happen to 'em, it would. Nothing I could do.

Clergyman: What do you expect from Christianity? A cheap escape from whatever frightens you?

Driver: Well, what is Jesus supposed to do?

Clergyman: He lets us in on Himself, on what He is and on what He does. He is YES to us, and He asks us to believe that and to give up our other "gods" and self-justifications. His best-known stories were about Himself, because He was accused of saying YES to people who didn't have much going for them socially or morally or religiously—whores and traitors. He told about a son who took his inheritance and left home.

Driver: Yeah, yeah, I know. "Prodigal son." Right?

Clergyman: Right. Jesus has a different way of dealing with rejected people. We might call it "forgiveness," but it does not come cheap. Jesus' death is His final and total commitment to us. He experienced the verdict—let it happen to Him.

The boy in Jesus' story got that kind of YES; it set him free to admit that he was wrong. We are given that YES in Jesus; it sets us free to say NO to our fake religions. The YES is stronger than the verdict, because when the verdict had done its worst, the YES overcame it.

Driver: I never heard it that way before.

Clergyman: But that's what Christians mean by "Gospel." We entrust ourselves to the YES in Jesus. We hold to that YES against the NO of life in history. Jesus makes us free—free to enjoy His gifts, like bowling and kids and work and the wife. We're no longer trapped into making gods out of them. We're free to be *for* them as Jesus is *for* us.

Driver: Well, where does church and praying fit into all this?

Clergyman: It helps if we first stop thinking that church is a building or a religious organization. Church is really what happens to people when the Gospel is happening to them and through them to other people. The words that Christians share with one another about Jesus as God the Forgiver are meant to set them free for one another and for all men.

Driver: Doesn't sound like any church I know.

1. Think about it. In what ways is the taxi driver right?

2. In what ways is he wrong?

3. How would you react differently than this pastor did?

4. Read **2 Corinthians 1:18–22.** What does it mean to you that Jesus is your YES?

5. Read **James 1:26–27; 2:14–17.** Can religion be just belief? Explain.

6. Can religion be only a collection of *right* works? Why or why not?

WHAT IS FAITH?

1. Describe the difference between a religion and a faith.

2. Ask your teacher to tell you a story about Blondin, a publicity-seeking tightrope walker. How could you relate the story of the tightrope walker to the difference between religion and faith?

3. When do you stand on the sidelines and cheer? When are you silent?

4. Describe a situation in which you *wished* you had said more (like this preacher did).

Ask God to give you a new boldness to share His love with others, especially those of faiths other than yours. May His peace and certainty fill you with joy in your sharing the Gospel wherever and whenever it might be.

REMEMBER

Always be prepared to give an answer to everyone who asks you to give the reason for the hope that you have. But do this with gentleness and respect, keeping a clear conscience, so that those who speak maliciously against your good behavior in Christ may be ashamed of their slander.

1 Peter 3:15–16

FOR NEXT TIME

If you had only two minutes to describe your faith to someone, what would you say? How much or how little would you include in your short statement of belief? Are there any already-prepared statements that you might use?

Session 2

What Is Christianity?

WHAT WOULD YOU SAY?

Wally came home from work late one night. As usual, he rode the bus. Suddenly he heard a thud and felt the bus lurch to an awkward halt. The driver ordered everyone out immediately. The curious passengers piled out quickly. The gathering crowd buzzed with excitement.

As Wally stepped out of the bus into the cold night air, he heard a woman ask, "What happened?"

"Some fellow got hit," one man replied in a gruff voice. "He's under there now," he continued, pointing under the bus.

"Why don't they move the bus off him?" the same woman pleaded.

"It would kill him immediately if they did," came the response from the same man, only softer this time. "I'm afraid he's stuck under there!"

The woman gasped, as she shivered against the chilling night air.

Wally knelt down, quietly surveyed the situation, and moved to the front of the bus. He saw a body pinned between the two wheels. Any movement of the bus would surely crush the already badly injured man, he thought. Wally heard the bus driver yelling for someone to call an ambulance and a tow truck.

Without hesitating, Wally crawled under the bus. To his amazement, he discovered that the man was conscious. Wally hadn't had much medical training beyond the Boy Scout First Aid Merit Badge and the little bit of First Aid in health class the previous semester. But inexperienced as he was, it was obvious to Wally that the man was near death.

Wally took a deep breath and began to talk. He spoke in a low, but distinct voice. Wally told the man . . .

Wait. Let's ask you. What would you have told the man if you had been Wally?

YOU DON'T SAY!

1. Maybe you wouldn't have crawled under the bus in the first place! Imagine instead that you watched someone else crawl under the bus, someone you *knew*

wasn't a Christian. What do you suppose that person would say to the dying man?

2. Ask yourself, "Could I say the same thing to that person?" Why or why not?

3. What if that non-Christian just talked about the weather—how cool it was that evening. Could you have said that? Why or why not?

4. Suppose that non-Christian crawled under the bus and tried to have the man sign an organ-donor card. Could you have done that?

5. Suppose he tried to encourage the person by saying, "Contemplate. Meditate. Simply believe you're out from under this bus, and it will be." Could you say that?

6. We Christians have a unique and very important message: Jesus. We are compelled to talk about Him **(Acts 4:20).** No, we don't always choose the time or place **(1 Peter 3:15).** But we are encouraged to do it with boldness. We are encouraged to share the *hope* that Jesus gives us!

Listen to what Peter said. **"Salvation is found in no one else, for there is no other name under heaven given to men by which we must be saved" (Acts 4:12).** Peter was talking to a group of people who were having a hard time believing. They couldn't quite accept the fact that Jesus truly was the Messiah who had risen from the dead. Peter was on trial for his life. He could have chosen to say nothing, but he sensed that people were dying—just like the person under the bus. Peter spoke up. He didn't mince words, either. He spoke about Jesus. Peter said, "Jesus is the only way to heaven." No ifs, ands, or buts!

How do these claims about Jesus Christ as the only way to heaven affect what you would have said under the bus?

7. Now go back to the bus situation. Why would you want yourself, instead of a non-Christian, to crawl under the bus?

YOU DO SAY!

Many think the main purpose of the Bible is to show us how to live. Those people make it a book of rules. But in **1 John 5:13** God tells us that the Bible is primarily meant to show us the way to heaven—to help us know *for sure* that we're going there. The Bible is God's Word *to us* to show us how to be saved (**2 Timothy 3:15–16**). God wants us to know that Jesus is the *only* way to heaven, just as Peter said in **Acts 4:12.**

Put yourself under the bus again. What would you tell the dying man? Would you talk about the weather? Would you ask about his church membership? Or would you talk to him about what God says in the Bible? Would you ask him about heaven and his relationship with Jesus? What would you say?

IT'S THE LEAST YOU COULD SAY

Think of a very good sermon you heard. Could you remember all of it? Do you think you could repeat it to the man under the bus? What if he didn't live that long? The ambulance and tow truck might arrive before you finished. He might not get to hear the best parts of the sermon.

Think about it. What's the very *least* that you could tell a dying person? Would you quote the Bible, or would you talk about Jesus in your own words?

Outline what you'd say in three or four short phrases. Write a brief summary of your Christian faith. Make it short—something you could easily remember. Then look at the outline and related Bible verses below.

1. Everyone is a sinner and in need of salvation (**Romans 3:23**).

2. God is both just and merciful and offers His grace freely (**Ephesians 2:8–9**).

3. Jesus came to earth to *redeem* us from our sins (**Galatians 4:4–5**).

If you wish, add your own notes in the margins.

What things would you say, or what comforting Bible verses would you like to quote?

YOU BET YOUR LIFE

Someone once described Christianity as "a leap of faith." It's like "leaping into the darkness, hoping God is there to catch you." Someone else said that it's like "putting all your eggs in one basket."

These definitions leave something to be desired. Compare them with the short summary of faith that you wrote.

Your summary will be especially important to you while you study other religions during the next few weeks. You'll want and need something with which to compare other religions. You'll want a short witness that you can share when asked to give account of the hope you have.

ON WHAT WOULD YOU BET YOUR LIFE?

Go back to that dying man under the bus. Suppose you disagreed with what the non-Christian said to him. Suppose, for example, that he was a Buddhist encouraging the dying person to reach toward Nirvana—a spiritual condition of perfect peace.

What could you say later to that Buddhist? Could you at least share your brief description of Christianity—what Jesus means to you—that He died for your sins and for theirs? "You can tell the love of Jesus; You can say He died for all" (*Lutheran Worship*, 318, stanza 2).

REMEMBER

Salvation is found in no one else, for there is no other name under heaven given to men by which we must be saved.

Acts 4:12

FOR NEXT TIME

Next time we will talk about how all organized religions seem to have some similarities, and yet have some differences. See how many you can list. (Hint: Do all religions have sacred writings? Do they all have a belief in a supreme being?)

Session 3

Who Cares What Others Believe, Anyway?

RELIGIONS: CREATE YOUR OWN

Do the following activity to help you understand people with non-Christian beliefs:

Divide your class into four groups. Each group should develop an original system of religious beliefs.

Begin by pretending you know nothing God has revealed to you in Scripture. You do not know that God created the world in six days. You do not know that Adam and Eve's sin spoiled that perfect creation . . . that God promised a Savior . . . that Jesus became a man . . . that He died and rose again . . . that heaven and hell exist . . . that the Holy Spirit gives you faith . . . that you cannot work your way into heaven . . .

Develop your "religion" from what you know as a human being and from what you see in the world around you.

As you develop your beliefs, you might consider the following:

1. When I was a young child and afraid of the dark or a storm, what were some things I imagined?

2. How did I get here?

3. What happens after I die?

4. Why do bad things happen?

5. Why do good things happen?

6. Is there some kind of a supreme being? If so, what is (are) he (she, they) like?

7. What happens if you are good?

8. What happens if you are bad?

RELIGIONS: SIMILAR AND DIFFERENT

1. Now summarize the system of religious beliefs that each group in your class developed. You might put some key points of each belief system on the chalkboard or chart paper.

2. Compare those belief systems. What are some similarities? What are some differences?

3. "Real" belief systems tend to have the similarities and differences listed below. How did your class's belief systems compare with them?

Similarities

Belief in a higher power
Sacred writings
People and places
Rituals
Golden rule

Differences

Ideas about sin or evil
Ideas about salvation
Ideas about a personal god

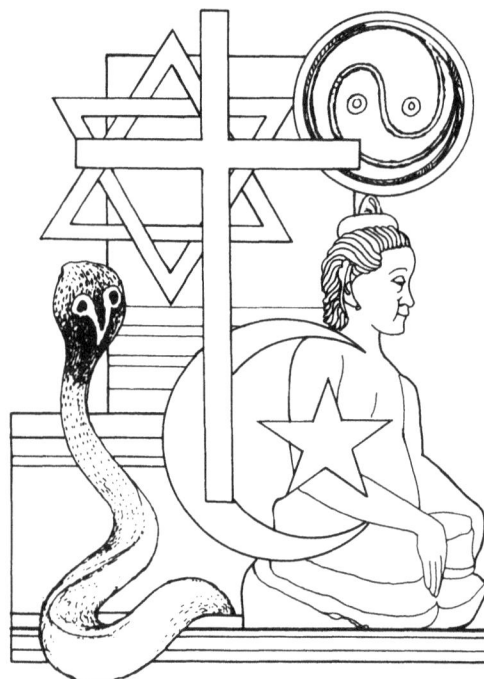

ONLY TWO RELIGIONS IN THE WORLD

In reality, only two religions exist in the world: the Christian religion and the non-Christian religion. If you followed the assignment as suggested, you developed a non-Christian religion. (Maybe this was hard, because you know Christ and His teachings so well. Without Scripture, however, you could *not* know Him.)

Compare your religious systems with Christianity:

1. Did a supreme being humble himself and get down to your level?

2. Did a supreme being die for you? and rise again?

3. Did a supreme being keep on loving you even when you abused him?

4. Did good things happen to you (for example, life after death) because of the love of a supreme being instead of as a result of things you did to *earn* them?

The following story illustrates, at least in a small way, the love Jesus has for you:

One day you went for a walk and fell into a very deep hole. You scratched and jumped, trying to get out, when you suddenly heard a noise in the corner. There, curled up, you saw a deadly, poisonous snake.

You screamed for help and received a lot of sympathy and encouragement, but no one helped you out.

Finally, Jesus Christ came along. He saw you in the hole and, without a word, jumped into the hole with you. The noise of Jesus boosting you out of the hole angered the snake, and it struck Jesus. Jesus fell dead, but you walked away free.

That's the difference between Christianity and all other religions in the world. Other religions leave you in the hole. They offer you ways to work yourself out on your own by meditating, contemplating, or trying hard to perfect yourself. Only Christians realize that Jesus Christ got into the hole of sin with all of us. He died to set us free from sin's bondage!

WHO CARES WHAT OTHERS BELIEVE, ANYWAY?

"I believe in Jesus. I know He loves me, forgives me, and will take me to heaven. I want everyone else to believe that, too. So I intend to tell people about Jesus. But I don't first have to learn what those people believe, do I? Can't I just go up to people and tell them about Jesus?"

Because of the power of the Holy Spirit, people *do* believe. God's Word works, even when the witness doesn't know the belief of the listener.

But people will often not listen to the message of God's love unless we present it in the context of their own experience. Furthermore, people tend to "turn us off" when we approach them with an attitude of "lording it over them."

Talk about effective witnessing. How will the experience of pretending to develop a new religious system help you witness more effectively to the Muslim who lives three blocks away, the Hindu who plays on your baseball team, or the Buddhist you will meet in college?

REMEMBER

Jesus answered, "I am the way and the truth and the life. No one comes to the Father except through Me."

John 14:6

FOR NEXT TIME

During the next five sessions we will talk about five major world religions: Hinduism, Buddhism, Confucianism, Islam, and Judaism. For next time, find information in books and encyclopedias about the Hindu religion. Look for magazine and newspaper articles about religious unrest in India, which has been prevalent in recent years. Perhaps you know relatives or friends who have visited India. Talk with them about what they have discovered about the people and their religions.

UNIT 2

World Religions The Big Five

For centuries people all over the world have sought answers to questions like

"Who am I?"

"Where did I come from?"

"Where am I going?"

"Is there really some kind of existence after this life?"

"How do you get there?"

Even though you know about Jesus Christ, you may have wondered about those same things at times.

Many others in the world have *not* heard about Jesus Christ. They may know His name, but they don't know that it means "Savior," the One who has taken away our sins. They have questions, and they are trying to answer them with their religions.

Their religions may be "older" than Christianity, but we know that *in Christ* God has revealed to us the truth about how to get close to Him. "Salvation is found in no one else, for there is no other name under heaven given to men by which we must be saved" (**Acts 4:12**).

As you go through the next five sessions, pay particular attention to ways you might be able to share *your* faith in Jesus with people who hold beliefs other than your own. You can respect the sincerity of their beliefs without agreeing with them.

Learn ways that others seek answers to life's important questions. Be sensitive to what they believe. Then pray for God's guidance, so that you can share your faith with them. Then you can rest comfortably, leaving conversion in the hands of God.

May your faith be enhanced as you learn about the faiths of others!

Session 4

Hinduism: One of the Oldest Religions

[Jesus said,] *"Come to Me, all you who are weary and burdened, and I will give you rest."*
Matthew 11:28

The roots of Hinduism predate Abraham. Therefore Hinduism is the oldest of the religions you will study in this unit.

Many people consider Christianity to be a young religion, based on its "birth" at Pentecost. However, the truths of our Christian faith are the same truths as those taught in the Old Testament, beginning with God's promise to Adam and Eve in **Genesis 3:15.** Thus one can say that Christianity actually predates Hinduism.

WHAT DO YOU KNOW ABOUT HINDUISM?

Before you study and discuss *Hinduism*, tell whether the following statements are true or false.

1. Hindus believe that their God, the Ultimate Reality, is never really knowable.

2. One of the main characteristics of Hinduism is that it claims to be the best expression of truth, and is therefore an exclusive religion.

3. Hindus believe they have lived before and will live again.

4. Hindus don't meditate with Yoga until they are near the end of their life.

5. Hindus try to become involved with life and to solve problems as much as they can. Thereby they know everything they need to know to get through life.

CHARACTERISTICS OF HINDUISM

Openness to and Absorption of All Other Religions

Hinduism is rather unique in that it is open to other religions and is able to absorb the religious beliefs and rituals of any other religion. Hindus see other religions as acceptable alternatives and equal roads to the same end. The end, or the Ultimate Reality (Brahman), is the basis for all being. Yet they believe it is not knowable by the mere human mind.

Extreme Complexity

Hinduism is part nature worship and part pantheism (God *is* nature). It's a worship of many, many gods. Yet at the same time, it requires no set worship pattern by any of its followers.

Hinduism talks of three main gods. Brahma is considered the creator; Vishnu, the sustainer; and Siva (or Shiva), the destroyer. Individual followers don't actually "belong" to a religion as such. They may worship when and where they choose. Whatever concept of God seems best for the individual is acceptable.

An Eternal Soul That Never Dies

Hindus believe that Atman is a kind of "master soul" from which all individuals come and to which everyone must return. Most individuals never become freed from the distractions of this world. They aren't able to reach a state of perfect peace (called "Nirvana") in one lifetime, since an individual isn't able to progress through all the states necessary to reach this Nirvana. Thus Hindus believe that the individual never really dies but is repeatedly reborn into different bodies.

The belief in reincarnation is not unique to this religion, though their caste system is.

Caste System

Hindus believe that each individual is born into a position in life that can never be changed. Four basic castes (levels) exist. (Many subcastes also exist but are too numerous to mention and too difficult to define without a lifelong acquaintance.)

1. *Brahmins* (priests and philosophers) are the upper caste group. They are the intellectual and spiritual leaders of the people.

2. *Kshatriyas* (administrators and politicians) are the second-highest group. They are involved in government and professional life.

3. *Vaisyas* (farmers and merchants) form the next caste group.

4. *Sudras* (laborers and servants) come next, on the last rung of the Hindu caste ladder.

5. The "untouchables" (social outcasts), though not originally a part of the caste system, are the people below the bottom of the ladder. These unfortunate people, are often scorned and mocked by others. Their only hope (at least until recent reforms) has been for death and reincarnation at a higher level in the caste system as their reward for having done jobs well.

Although the caste system has been outlawed by the government, it continues to be an important part of the social system in India.

Separation by Meditation

Hindus journey toward the state of perfect peace (they believe), separating themselves from worldly distractions. They do this through Yoga, a kind of meditation. Hindus believe that there are four kinds of people, corresponding to the four states of life. They believe that each kind of person needs a different kind of yoga.

A person is first a learner, progressing to the second stage (marrying and having a family). From there, a Hindu hopes to pass to a third stage (mature self-understanding). The fourth and last stage (Sannyism) is a prolonged spiritual examination. During this time the individual prepares to enter the first stage again in his or her next reincarnation.

A person's "karma" (whole set of thoughts and deeds) is added together to determine what the next incarnation will be. Hindus believe that how well they handled their lives this time around determines whether they move to a higher or lower level.

Hindu Scriptures

Hindu sacred writings were first collected between 1500 and 800 B. C. Believing these revelations to be inspired, the Hindu scriptures indicate divine will to different people in different life cycles. The *Vedas* are four collections of prayers, rituals, and hymns. The *Upanishads* are a collection of philosophical and theological arguments and commentaries on life.

Individual Worship

Since worship for the Hindu is individual, a follower may worship whenever and wherever he or she wishes. Flowing water is significant both as a symbol of the ever-flowing knowledge of God and as a place of revelation.

WHAT DOES THE BIBLE SAY?

Read the following Bible passages. List ways in which Christianity is *the same as* or *different from* Hinduism.

Exodus 20:3–6
Matthew 6:7
Matthew 28:19
John 3:16
Ephesians 2:8–9
Hebrews 9:27

WHAT WOULD YOU SAY?

Write a brief response to Hinduism.
- What do you think about Hinduism as you have come to know it?
- How do you think you would begin to share your Christian faith with a person of Hindu belief?
- What could you say to a Hindu about the comfort you have in knowing beyond a doubt that you have eternal life?
- Think about the certainty that you have because of Christ's death and resurrection for *you!* How could this help direct you in sharing with a Hindu? How might this cause difficulty for you?

REMEMBER

The Word became flesh and made His dwelling among us. We have seen His glory, the glory of the One and Only, who came from the Father, full of grace and truth.

John 1:14

FOR NEXT TIME

Discover how Buddhism grew out of Hinduism. Make a list of things you now know about Buddhism.

Session 5

Who Is the Enlightened One— Buddha or Christ?

JESUS CARES

Jesus said, . . . *"If anyone would come after Me, he must deny himself and take up his cross and follow Me."*

Matthew 16:24

WHAT DO YOU KNOW ABOUT BUDDHISM?

Which statements do you think are true?

1. Buddhism is not distinct from Hinduism.

2. Buddhism is not widely accepted in the country of its origin.

3. Buddha taught that happiness lies within each person and his or her capacities.

4. Buddhism has no supernatural authority and contains no rituals.

5. The name "Buddha" means "The Enlightened One."

The belief system of Buddhism began through the spiritual insights of Siddhartha Gautama, who lived from about 560 to 480 B.C. Raised as a Hindu, Gautama enjoyed benefits that were his as a child of a clan chief.

When Gautama was born, a prophet said that if this child lived at home, he would be a great king. If he left home, he would become a kind of savior. To keep him from leaving, his father surrounded him with riches and comfort. He kept all painful, sad, and ugly sights from him.

Gautama married and had a child, but remained a prisoner within his father's castle all the while. One day he told his father that he wanted to see the rest of the world. His father reluctantly prepared for his travel by ordering that the city streets be cleaned and that all diseased and old people be removed from the streets.

Understandably, some of the sick and infirm didn't get the message. Young Gautama referred to things he saw as "the four passing sights." **This awakening incident marked a drastic change in Gautama's attitudes and life.**

First he saw an old man. He was told that everyone in the world would someday become old.

Next he saw a sick man. He was made aware that everyone was likely at one time or another to become sick.

Then he watched people carrying a corpse to be cremated and thrown into the Ganges River. He was informed that this was the end for each living person.

Finally, he saw a monk begging for food. The peaceful expression on this man's face convinced Gautama that this was the life he sought.

Gautama left his wife and child and studied for seven years after his 29th birthday. He meditated on the answers to all of the questions that had arisen in his mind since he observed the four passing sights. He wanted to find the perfect peace that he had seen on the begging monk's face. As he meditated one day, he had what was later called his "great enlightenment."

Gautama immediately taught five others, who became monks. He began his ministry on the banks of the sacred Ganges River in the city of Benares. His preaching not only marked the beginning of a major world religion but also provided the basis for all other Buddhist teachings.

Gautama's followers regarded him as the "Enlightened One," so they referred to him as *Buddha.*

Buddha said he found a "middle path" between completely indulging all desires and complete denial (or asceticism). He taught his followers to reach for this path by subscribing to the "four noble truths," which climaxed in the "eightfold path to goodness."

The noble truths were *the existence of suffering, the cause of suffering, the end of suffering,* and *the end of all pain* (by following the eightfold path: *right views, right resolve, right speech, right behavior, right occupation, right effort, right contemplation,* and *right meditation*). Although few complete all eight, those who do are said to have reached "nirvana" (the state of complete enlightenment; the state of complete absence of every thought and desire).

After Buddha's death, some considered him a divine being. But this belief is not essential to being a Buddhist. Most Buddhists do not accept belief in any supreme being.

Buddhism is divided into several branches, depending on the severity of the discipline: *Theravada Buddhism, Mahayana Buddhism, Tantric Buddhism,* and *Zen Buddhism* (not really Buddhism, but for some a "completion" of Buddhism, much as Christianity might be considered to be a completion of Judaism).

The main teachings of Buddhism are contained in the "Ten Buddhist Precepts." Only the first five are required of those who choose not to become monks.

- Kill no living thing, including insects.
- Do not steal.
- Do not commit adultery.
- Tell no lies.
- Do not drink intoxicants or take drugs.
- Eat moderately and only at the appointed time.
- Avoid that which excites the senses.
- Do not wear adornments (including perfume).
- Do not sleep in luxurious beds.
- Accept no silver or gold.

Compare these teachings with those of Christianity. How are they different? In what ways are they the same? Could you follow these precepts?

THE CORE OF BUDDHISM

Buddhism is concerned with people, not with God. Buddhism is concerned with how people handle the things that happen to them and not with why things happen. It's concerned about the value an individual Buddhist finds in life, and not with the value of life itself.

How do you react to these Buddhist ideas?

COMPARING CHRISTIANITY AND BUDDHISM

What does it mean to be protected "from the world"? Think about how God has or has not done this for you.

Buddha went into a sad, ugly, sick world after years of his father's protection from it all. What are some ways you might try to protect others from the world's ugliness? Do you think this is what Jesus wants us to do? What "protection" can we offer people through Christ?

When Jesus tells us to deny ourselves **(Matthew 16:24),** what do you think He means? How does that compare to Buddhist ideas?

When Jesus said, **"Take up your cross"** (Matthew **16:24),** He referred to the suffering of the cross that He endured, and similar pain that we might be asked to bear for Him **(Philippians 3:10).**

Now read **Romans 5:3.** What often happens through suffering? If we aren't built up, what often happens? What could be done to keep our faith from weakening?

WHAT CAN YOU LEARN?

Buddhists spend much time meditating and denying themselves worldly pleasures. What are their motives? Who is doing the action?

What about you? Might you spend more time in personal devotions and self-denial? If so, how would you differ from a Buddhist? Are you trying to save yourself or do you have a desire to learn more about God and to do His will?

Ask God for the power of the Spirit to keep you strong in the Christian faith and to celebrate the victory Christ has won for you. Ask Him to guide and direct your words and actions so that when you meet people struggling under a set of human rules, you can offer them the Good News of salvation in Jesus and joy and happiness forever.

REMEMBER

We also rejoice in our sufferings, because we know that suffering produces perseverance; perseverance, character; and character, hope. And hope does not disappoint us, because God has poured out His love into our hearts by the Holy Spirit, whom He has given us.

Romans 5:3–5

FOR NEXT TIME

Read about Confucianism. You've probably heard a "Confucius say . . . " story or joke. What aspect of this religion leads to these stories or jokes?

Session 6

The Wisdom of the Ancients Confucianism

HOW SMART ARE YOU?

Perhaps you have heard the quote, often attributed to Mark Twain: "When I was 18, I thought my father to be the most stupid man in the world. When I reached 21, I couldn't figure out how he had learned so much in just three short years." How do you think Mark Twain's father felt toward him when he was 18? How about when he reached 21?

How do you think God feels toward people who have wisdom but don't have Jesus? What is the only thing that will change God's attitude of wrath toward people? What wisdom do you find in **John 15:5?** in **Hebrews 11:6?**

What, really, is wisdom? Is it a desire to follow Someone who was murdered by an angry mob? Doesn't that seem more like foolishness? No wonder that many intellectual people view Christianity as a bad joke!

God has given us quite a task, hasn't He? He calls upon us to bring our "foolish" message to those people so they will grow up and see His wisdom. Pray that they will. May God use your work and witness to bring them to faith in Him.

Confucianism is a religion of the world's wisdom today. For 300 million people in China, it is *the* way of life. Pray that the Spirit of the living God will use the 2 million Christians living there to witness to the truth of Jesus.

HOW MUCH DO YOU KNOW?

Which of the following statements do you think are true?

1. The religions of China and Japan are more concerned about "the way of life" than they are about God.

2. Chinese philosophy pictures all of human life as having a pattern that can be detected and lived out.

3. Confucius encouraged people to admire musicians, artists, poets, and teachers more than soldiers.

4. Confucianism has never been recognized as a significant religion in China.

5. One of the main goals of Confucius was to de-

velop principles whereby people might restore peace in the world.

CONFUCIUS THE MAN

Confucius was born about 550 B. C. in present-day Shantung, China, during a time of total chaos. Government officials sanctioned raids by military forces that thought it better to kill their prisoners than to imprison them. One macabre story recounts victims being flung into boiling cauldrons, with the survivors being forced to eat this human soup. Confucius believed that China could be saved, if only the people would seek the good of others, as their ancestors had taught. After his death, some elevated Confucius to the position of a god, but not in the same sense as we believe in God.

ANCESTOR WORSHIP

Confucius, because of his respect for the teachings of his ancestors, encouraged their worship. He said that the continued existence of the ancestors' spirits depends on the attention given them by their living relatives. He also taught that the ancestors can control the fortunes of their families. This has become one of the main teachings of Confucianism. Although Confucius did believe in a place where the spirits of the dead lived after death, this belief was not accompanied by a corresponding belief in a supreme being.

As a result of this unusual teaching, many people live in fear of their ancestors. They believe that if they faithfully remember their departed relatives, good will come their way. They attribute bad fortune to the neglect of the dead.

RESPECT OF THE ELDERS

Long before the time of Confucius a kind of filial piety existed in China. The younger members of the family were required to pay their respects—bordering on worship—to the "gray-haired" group. It was especially required that a son respect his father.

This teaching was so well received, because all figured they would one day be old and receive the same kind of respect. They also knew they would receive great reverence after they died.

SIX DOCTRINAL PRINCIPLES OF CONFUCIANISM

Confucianism can be summarized in six key terms or ways.

1. Jen—the Golden Rule. Jen is the idea of humaneness, goodness, and helpfulness toward others. It is the foundation of everything that follows. If everyone would practice this principle, the world would achieve peace and harmony.

2. Chunt-tzu—Being the Real Person. A person who takes the abstract idea of Jen and makes it a daily habit is considered to be "chun-tzu," a gentleman, man at his best. It means having such a right attitude that it flows out into action no matter what the circumstance. This kind of person can transform society, according to Confucius.

3. Cheng-Ming—Proper Names. All are to act their proper part. A king should act like a king, a gentleman like a gentleman. A person's name is extremely important in that it dictates the kind of behavior that person should exhibit.

4. Li—the Right Pattern. Li has several different meanings, depending on the context. It can mean doing things properly, or with correct reverence or courtesy. It can also mean using the correct ritual or standard of conduct. It is all very complicated for westerners, who aren't even sure which people to address by first names! Especially important for Confucius were the re-lationships between family members—father to son, older brother to younger brother, husband to wife, etc. According to Confucianism, these are the basic building blocks of any society.

5. Te—Government by Moral Power. "Te" literally means "power." The power to rule consists in more than just the physical power. The ruler needs to be virtuous and to inspire the subjects to follow. Obviously, according to the rule of the worship of ancestors, present leaders are to follow the pattern of successful rulers of the past and worship them.

6. Wen—Cultivation of the Peaceful Arts. Confucius held the peaceful arts in high esteem. These include poetry, music, and art. He felt that these, which came from the earlier Chou period, were symbols of virtue that should be maintained throughout the culture. Confucius condemned the culture in which he lived because it lacked virtue.

CONFUCIANISM AND CHRISTIANITY

1. Confucianism contains a great deal of wisdom and encourages good ethical training, but it also stresses the effort of the individual. What is wrong with this? What does God say about human nature (**Romans 6:23; Ephesians 2:1–5**)?

2. Confucianism encourages people to worship the ancients and follow their way. What are dangers of respecting people too highly? (See, for example, **Acts 12:19–23.**)

REMEMBER

The message of the cross is foolishness to those who are perishing, but to us who are being saved, it is the power of God. For it is written: "I will destroy the wisdom of the wise; the intelligence of the intelligent I will frustrate."

1 Corinthians 1:18–19

FOR NEXT TIME

Learn something about Islam. Why is it the fastest-growing religion in the world today? Why do you think that Islam has had such a great impact on world politics in recent decades?

Session 7

The Fastest-Growing Religion: Islam

PILGRIMS IN A FOREIGN LAND

Imagine being in a crowded airport. From the people arriving, the festive garments, and the happy atmosphere they project, you know that some sort of celebration is about to take place. You recognize people from many different lands and cultures. You have heard several languages you don't understand. An event of far-reaching significance must be about to begin.

You could be at an airport of a large metropolitan city in the United States just before Christmas or Easter. Or you could be at the airport in Jidda, Saudi Arabia, together with thousands of Muslims making their *hajj*—their required once-in-a-lifetime pilgrimage to the sacred city of Mecca, the birthplace of Muhammad, founder of the Muslim faith, called Islam. Maybe you know about Christians who have taken a pilgrimage to Bethlehem, the birthplace of their Savior. In this way we find a similarity between Christianity and the Muslim faith. Also, Muslims and Christians each believe in one God and also honor the prophets.

Jesus asks all people to consider who He is. With Peter, we can say, **"You are the Christ, the Son of the living God" (Matthew 16:16).** As we witness to people, who (like the Muslims) also seek the truth, may we be faithful to God's Word and ways. May those people one day trust in Jesus and join us in the everlasting choir in heaven!

HOW MUCH DO YOU KNOW?

Which of the following statements are true?

1. According to Muslims, Muhammad is the last of God's prophets.

2. Islam is a mixture of Judaism and Christianity.

3. Islam's theological system is very complicated.

4. The Black Muslims are a group of black Islamic believers who organized themselves during the time of racial difficulties in the United States.

THE PROPHET AND THE NAME

Muhammad was born about A. D. 570 in Mecca, Arabia (now in Saudi Arabia). At the age of 25 he married a wealthy widow, Khadija, 15 years older than himself.

He had some early contacts with both Christian and Jewish people. Muhammad's preaching reveals some knowledge of Christianity, but he rejected the central doctrines, such as the deity of Christ, His atoning death on the cross, and the Trinity.

Muhammad was profoundly dissatisfied with the polytheism and crude superstitions of the people of his area, and would retire to caves for seclusion, fasting, and meditation. During these times he became convinced of the existence of only one God.

Muhammad's later desire to conquer the world for Allah resulted from a kind of war that was raging within him. He was a peace-loving man, yet he felt an urgency to establish a world community before God's judgment destroyed it. He would later justify the use of the sword to establish such a kingdom.

THE WRITING

He claimed no miracles or infallibility for himself, but Muhammad believed that God (Arabic: *Allah*) had appointed him to carry the truth to the world. The real miracle, Muhammed felt, was the Qur'an—"reading" or "recitation." This Qur'an (or Koran), though compiled after Muhammad's death, came from his notes and oral teachings. Faithful followers feel that these are the very words of Allah.

The entire Koran may be summarized in the creed, "There is no God but God [Allah], and Muhammad is his prophet." These words are the motto text of Muslim homes, their baptismal formula, and the final message for the dying. By this creed the faithful are called to prayer five times daily. It forms the platform for unity for all the warring sects of Islam.

Muslims respect the Bible, but accept its teachings only as they are interpreted by the Qur'an. Muhammad believed that the Bible was altered, and that Jesus never died and rose again. (Judas was crucified in His place.) The Bible was revealed to people who were immature and incapable of understanding the wisdom of God, people who also have corrupted it in its transmission from one generation to another.

THE TEACHINGS OF ISLAM

The Qur'an describes Allah as all-powerful and all-knowing, who does as he pleases. Although he is described as vengeful and sometimes acting rather arbitrarily, he is also said to be merciful and compassionate. Forgiveness depends on right belief and good works. There is a great deal of uncertainty as to what measure of works is acceptable to Allah. Those who truly accept Islam desire to do what the name means, "surrender."

Islam may be summarized in five or six "pillars," or demands, required of its adherents.

1. The Creed, or *shahadah.* It is spoken often each day. Muslims hope that at least once during their lifetimes they will repeat it correctly and with heartfelt thanks.

2. The Ritual Prayers, *salat.* They are spoken along with the creed five times a day, always bowing toward Mecca. These prayers help people learn the most important lesson—that we are not God! Since all Muslims participate in these set prayer times, a worldwide fellowship is created even when a Muslim is isolated physically.

3. Almsgiving or charity, *zakat.* Each Muslim is *required* to donate 2½% of all possessions (rather than just income) to causes that the individual feels are worthy. Additional amounts may be given on a *voluntary* basis.

4. Fasting, *sawm.* Muslims are required to abstain from food, drink, and sexual intercourse from sunrise to sunset during the month of Ramadan. (Since Muslims follow a lunar calendar, the months rotate among the seasons. This demand becomes especially difficult when Ramadan falls during summer.)

5. The Pilgrimage to Mecca, *hajj.* This is required at least once during one's lifetime if the individual can possibly make it. It is said to remind all people of their equality with all other people and their devotion to Allah.

To these five main "pillars" of Islam, Shi'ite Muslims add a sixth.

6. Exertion, *jihad.* Reactionary groups believe that they must exert themselves as much as possible to remove all obstacles to spreading Islam worldwide.

HOSTILITY BETWEEN ISLAM AND CHRISTIANITY

Through the centuries the conflict between Islam and Christianity has been marked by combat (for example, during the Crusades). At other times, however, people on both sides have sought peace.

But Christianity can never compromise with a religion that denies the deity of Christ. We can hope for increased understanding and respect between the two religions. We can strive toward greater peace and a bolder witness to our faith in Jesus. We proclaim Jesus' death for all people, including those who, in the name of Muhammad, seek God too. We can share our faith in Jesus, hoping that someday it will become their faith too!

REMEMBER

[Jesus] asked His disciples, "Who do people say the Son of Man is?" ... Simon Peter answered, "You are the Christ, the Son of the living God."
Matthew 16:13, 16

FOR NEXT TIME

Using your Old Testament, find what you think are the beginnings of Judaism. Using the New Testament, look for passages that point out the center of the conflict between Jesus and the Judaism of His day.

Session 8

The Lord Our God Is One Lord: Judaism

THE CREED OF ISRAEL

Hear, O Israel: The Lord our God, the Lord is one.
Deuteronomy 6:4

BEGINNINGS OF ISRAEL

What things from the Old Testament do you remember about the beginnings of the Jews?

Since Christianity has the same historical roots as the nation of Israel, these should be familiar to you. What are the main teachings of the Jewish people?

CONFLICTS WITH JESUS

What do you remember from the New Testament about conflicts between the Jewish leaders and Jesus? What was their main complaint about Jesus?

HOW MUCH DO YOU KNOW?

Which of the statements below are true? Why?

1. Followers of Judaism believe they are partners with God in a two-way relationship of faithfulness.

2. Jewish people believe that God is faithful to His covenant, even when they are not.

3. Followers of Judaism today still hope for the Messiah.

4. The destruction of Jerusalem in A. D. 70 has had a profound effect on the customs of Judaism ever since.

5. Jewish people are easily converted to Christianity, since we have much of the Bible in common.

JUDAISM THEN

Judaism differs from the other religions we have studied in that it shares common roots with Christianity. Thus, we can look to Scripture to learn about its history through the time of St. Paul.

Stephen, the first Christian martyr, summarized much of that history in his speech to the Sanhedrin **(Acts 7:2–53).**

1. Read **verses 2–8.** What are some things about Abraham that stand out in your mind? Of what blessings are you reminded as you review the Abraham account?

2. Read **verses 9–19.** What are some things you recall about Joseph and about Israel's slavery in Egypt? What evidences of God's goodness do you find even in this account?

3. Read **verses 20–35.** What were some highlights of the first 80 years of Moses' life? What comfort do we still today get from God's words to Moses **(verse 34)?**

4. Read **verse 36.** Stephen used only one verse to summarize a major incident in Israel's history—an incident regarded by Old Testament people as perhaps the greatest evidence of God's mighty hand. Why is that incident still important to us today?

5. Read **verses 37–43.** In addition to telling about God's deliverance, Stephen spoke about some who rejected the leadership God had provided. Who else rejected God **(verses 51–52)?**

6. Read **verses 44–50.** Why were the tabernacle and temple important to the Old Testament people? What do you know about abuses that had crept into temple worship at the time of Christ? Why do we not need to continue the rituals God had ordered for the tabernacle and temple?

7. Read **verses 51–53.** What are some things you remember that illustrate the rejection of Jesus by leaders of the Jewish faith? What warnings for us do these verses suggest?

8. A few years after Stephen's death Paul brought the message of Christ to many places in his world. The Judaizers were almost a constant thorn to his ministry. Read **Galatians 3:1–5** and **5:1–12.** How were the Judaizers misleading some of the new Christians? What temptations to legalism have you had to face?

JUDAISM TODAY

Through the ages Judaism has changed in many ways. The Jews were known first as Hebrews **(Genesis 14:13),** and later as the people of Israel **(Genesis 32:28).** The term *Jew* comes from Judaism **(2 Maccabees 2:21 (22); 8:1**—an apocryphal book that tells about the movement).

Judaism today can be divided into three main groups: Orthodox, Conservative, and Reform.

Orthodox Jews interpret the Old Testament literally and strictly observe all 613 laws they find there.

Conservative Judaism, the largest group in the United States, observes the customs and Law, but only as it seems reasonable to them. They do keep the strict dietary laws, as do the Orthodox, but use more English and less Hebrew in their worship services.

Reform Judaism allows for each individual to interpret the meaning of their lives. They accept as binding only the moral laws of the Bible. They feel that the other customs and rules are incompatible with our modern civilization.

Modern Jews still celebrate many of the same festivals as their ancestors did, such as the Passover, Pentecost, the Feast of Weeks, and the Feast of Booths. The most important day of their year is Yom Kippur, or the Day of Atonement. On this day they celebrate the high priest's annual visit to the Holy of Holies in the temple to make a sacrifice for their sins **(Numbers 29:7–11).**

Jews are awaiting a Messianic age. Some look for a time when warring animals can peacefully coexist **(Isaiah 11:6–9).** Others wait for the Messiah to come.

We know that the Messiah has come. Jesus came, died, and rose again. In His blood we have forgiveness for all of our sins **(Romans 3:25).** We do not await His first coming, but His final coming, when He will take us to Himself in heaven, to live with Him forever. With our Jewish friends, spiritual cousins, we say, "**Hear, O Israel: The Lord our God, the Lord is one**" (Deuteronomy 6:4). And we witness our faith in this one God—Father, Son, and Holy Spirit—hoping that we someday might be one with our Jewish friends!

REMEMBER

It is for freedom that Christ has set us free. Stand firm, then, and do not let yourselves be burdened again by a yoke of slavery.
Galatians 5:1

FOR NEXT TIME

Plan to review the first eight sessions. You may wish to look ahead to Unit 3, where we will be looking at Christian religions, especially as they exist in the United States today.

Session 9

Review of Sessions 1–8

Give brief, yet complete, answers to the following questions.

1. What is a religion?

2. Respond to someone who says, "All religions are alright if you are sincere."

3. Name ways in which religions are somewhat similar.

4. Name three ways in which religions basically differ.

5. If someone asked you, "Why are you studying different religions in your class at a Lutheran high school?" how would you answer (aside from the fact that everyone has to take religion)?

6. Explain the statement, "There are only two religions in the world."

7. Which Bible passages that you know from memory are most important to you when sharing your faith in Jesus Christ with others?

8. What seems to you to be the most complex thing about Hinduism?

9. What about Hinduism makes you want to witness about Jesus to them?

10. Explain the difference between the meditation you do and that done by a Hindu.

11. What's wrong with the Hindu caste system?

12. How does the Buddhist claim to be saved?

13. What is nirvana?

14. How did Buddha reach enlightenment?

15. Explain the difference in motives between denial for a Christian and for a Buddhist.

16. Briefly describe Confucianism.

17. What are *yin* and *yang*?

18. Give examples of the kind of wisdom taught by Confucius.

19. Was Confucianism ever declared the state religion of China?

20. About when did Muhammad live?

21. What is the *hajj*?

22. What Christian source of comfort is missing in the Islamic faith?

23. Name at least one incident from history that could cause the Muslims to feel hostility toward Christians.

24. What part did Abraham have in the founding of God's covenant?

25. Why did God send Moses, rather than another Egyptian, to deliver the Israelites from Egypt?

26. Explain the significance of the Passover for the Jews and for Christians.

27. How has Judaism changed from the time of Christ until now?

28. Explain some sensitivies we must be aware of in order to witness effectively to Jewish people.

UNIT 3

"I Am the Way" Christian Religions

Have you ever driven down the street and noticed all the different church buildings? Do you wonder what goes on inside of them? How different are their worship services from yours? Do they sing the same hymns? Perhaps you've visited a church of another denomination. Were you surprised?

Why are there so many denominations? Their similarities and differences seem confusing at times, don't they? During this unit you will learn about some of those similarities and differences.

As we study various Christian denominations, let's remember that Jesus Christ proclaimed Himself as *the Way* (**John 14:6**). Doctrines of all Christian denominations will agree with that truth. Therefore, as you talk with other Christians, you will have a common starting point. That starting point is related to a goal you might set for yourself—to help other Christians see *the Way* more clearly.

Sometimes we let our human logic prevent us from believing everything God tells us in the Bible. Sometimes we set up human rules that get in the way of God's Word. Such unfortunate activities have led to the formation of all sorts of Christian denominations. When you learn about those things that "get in the way of *the Way*," God may give you new ideas for helping others see the grace of God. He freely makes *all* of us His sons and daughters. Let's celebrate that marvelous grace!

Session 10

The Great Schism: Roman Catholic Orthodox Traditions

CATHOLIC

What does the word catholic mean to you? Maybe you think of a Catholic church. It's really the Roman Catholic Church. The word catholic actually means universal or "worldwide." The church came to be known as "catholic" because until A. D. 1054 there was only one Christian church in the whole world.

A division had been growing between the eastern and western portions of the church for years, but it became final and official in 1054. Assembled in a council, church leaders in the eastern half of the empire declared that the churches in the western half of the empire were not teaching correct doctrine. The East excommunicated the West as heretics and declared themselves to be orthodox—"of the straight way." Shortly afterward, the West excommunicated the East. The Eastern segment was known as the "Orthodox" church; churches in the West held to the name catholic or universal. Gradually the term Roman Catholic was identified with the Western church, since it was headquartered in Rome.

BRIEF HISTORY OF THE ROMAN CATHOLIC CHURCH

The Roman Catholic Church believes that its roots lie in the small community of believers surrounding Jesus during His ministry on earth. Traditional beginnings of the papacy center on Peter and are based primarily on **Matthew 16:13–20.** When Jesus asked His disciples, **"Who do people say the Son of Man is?"** Peter responded, **"You are the Christ, the Son of the living God."** Jesus then told Peter, **" . . . On this rock I will build My church . . . . I will give you the keys of the kingdom of heaven . . . ."**

Certainly Peter *was* an important leader of the infant church **(Mark 5:37; 9:2; 14:33, 54; John 21:15–17; Acts 2:14; 3:6, 12; 4:8; 5:3, 15, 29; 11:4; and 12:3),** but we do not even have good historical evidence to support the view that he was a bishop of the church in Rome. Furthermore, God clearly states that He founded His church on God, and not on any human

(Ephesians 2:20). The rock on which Jesus would build His church was Peter's confession, **"You are the Christ, the Son of the living God" (Matthew 16:16),** and not the man Peter. Thus Scripture rejects a papacy built on Peter.

After its beginnings in Jerusalem, Christian congregations were formed in other cities as Paul and others spread the Gospel. Chief among these cities were Rome in Italy, Alexandria in Egypt, and Antioch in Syria. In 330, when the Roman emperor Constantine moved the center of his empire to Byzantium (now Istanbul, Turkey), and renamed the city Constantinople (for himself), it became another important center of Christianity.

Increasingly Constantine and succeeding emperors used the church to strengthen their control. The distinction between church and state became blurred. The emperor and the pope often wielded just about the same power. The congregation in Rome was the most powerful in the western part of the empire. The bishop of the church in Rome was called "pope," after the Latin word for "father." In time the pope came to be called the leader of the visible church on earth and claimed an unbroken line of succession back to the apostle Peter.

ROMAN CATHOLIC TEACHINGS

Many teachings of the Roman Catholic Church are quite similar to those of Lutherans. These include belief in a Trinity, the full humanity and deity of Jesus Christ, the Bible as the Word of God, and Baptism and Holy Communion as sacraments.

Other Roman Catholic teachings, however, differ from Lutheran teachings. Official Roman Catholic doctrine is that the bread and wine in Holy Communion are *transformed into* the body and blood of Christ. Since the very body and blood of Christ are present on the altar, they believe that Christ is "sacrificed" anew each time Holy Communion (the Mass) is celebrated. Scripture teaches, however, that Christ's one sacrifice is complete for all **(Hebrews 7:27; 1 Peter 3:18).**

Roman Catholics also elevated the popes to the

position of infallible leaders. Similarly, they elevated the position of the Virgin Mary and other saints and eventually taught that Mary was taken up bodily into heaven. Certainly we may honor Mary as the mother of the Lord. But she, like all other humans, was sinful and suffered temporal death. Other "saints" were also sinful and were all equally in need of a Savior. (Actually, a saint is *anyone* who believes in the Lord Jesus as Savior from sin—**Romans 1:7.**)

Official Roman Catholic teaching (Council of Trent, 1545-63) also speaks of a place called purgatory: "Since the Catholic Church . . . has . . . taught . . . that there is a purgatory . . . the holy council commands . . . that the sound doctrine of purgatory . . . be believed and maintained . . . and be everywhere taught and preached" (*Canons and Decrees of the Council of Trent,* Session XXV, 1563). Because the idea of purgatory suggests that believers still need to be purified from sin when they die, this teaching insults the perfect blood atonement of Christ on the cross. Other Roman Catholic teachings hold that works are necessary for salvation. The Bible teaches, however, that we are saved by grace alone, through faith in Jesus—a key teaching of Luther at the time of the Reformation.

Some changes have occurred in the Roman church during recent years. For example, the Second Vatican Council (1962–65) suggested changes that affect the way individual Catholics worship and react to other Christians. However, while the Roman church may be more willing to listen to other Christians, the above issues—and others—still separate Roman Catholics and Lutherans.

THE ORTHODOX CHURCH

The Eastern Orthodox Church had its own development after the "Great Schism," or split, in 1054. On the one hand, this church has retained much of the ceremony and hierarchy of the Roman church. On the other hand, the Orthodox church has been somewhat isolated from the rest of Christendom. The act of excommunicating the West began this isolation, and differences in language, culture, and politics have continued to encourage it. The Orthodox churches also suffered persecution as the Moslem Turks gained control over much of their land, and later under Communism.

Divided into several different branches according to locality (Greek, Russian, etc.), the Eastern Orthodox church also traces its existence to the apostles. Unlike their Roman Catholic counterparts, Orthodox priests may marry and raise families. Like the Roman church, the Orthodox church accepts seven sacraments. The Orthodox church also baptizes babies, but it does so by immersing the infant three times. Communicants in the Orthodox church receive bread that has been dipped into wine by "intinction."

Like the Roman and many Protestant churches, the Orthodox church accepts the Nicene Creed, except for the phrase, "and the Son" in the Third Article. Orthodox Christians believe that the Holy Spirit proceeds from the Father alone, and not from the Son. This disagreement, together with political pressures for supremacy, precipitated the "Great Schism" of 1054.

WHAT DO WE DO?

Roman Catholic and Orthodox beliefs differ from the beliefs of the religions in unit 2, primarily because Catholics and Orthodox Christians confess Jesus Christ as the way to salvation. When we witness to members of these denominations, we might begin with statements that encompass the common elements of our faith. As we do this, we need to avoid all temptations to compromise certain Biblical teachings just to have a closer fellowship.

We need to be careful when talking with individuals from these denominations, for the statements made in this session apply to the official teachings of their churches. Beliefs of individuals and teachings within congregations vary somewhat, especially since the Second Vatican Council. Instead of criticizing an individual for praying to Mary or believing in purgatory, we might focus on the joy we feel because Jesus has completely atoned for all our sins and freely offers us eternal life.

REMEMBER

No one can say, "Jesus is Lord," except by the Holy Spirit.

1 Corinthians 12:3

FOR NEXT TIME

See how many church reformers you can name. Try to connect them to particular church bodies that exist today. What evidence of their beliefs do you find in those churches?

Session 11

The Reformation: Roots of Protestantism

It is by grace you have been saved, through faith—and this not from yourselves, it is the gift of God—not by works, so that no one can boast.

Ephesians 2:8–9

WHEN DID THE PROTESTANT REFORMATION BEGIN?

Historians generally use Oct. 31, 1517, as the date the Protestant Reformation began. On that day a young monk, Martin Luther, nailed 95 theses to the door of the Castle Church in Wittenberg, Germany.

Actually, others with similar dreams of reformation lived before Luther. John Wycliffe and John Hus had dreamed of a church with teachings based on the Word of God. People like Zwingli, a contemporary of Luther, worked for a church free of objects that reminded them of the Roman Catholics. People like Calvin and Knox became "second generation reformers," influential in forming the various denominations. Still later came Wesley, founder of Methodism.

WYCLIFFE

John Wycliffe, a professor at Oxford, lived in 14th century England. One of the hottest issues for discussion in his day was that of "dominion" or "lordship." While most theologians agreed that lordship came from God, they disagreed how it was transmitted to people. The Roman church taught that the absolute rulership of the church had been conferred to a succession of popes who, in the exercise of their office, were thought to have authority that extended to every element of daily life.

Wycliffe insisted that the relationship between God and His people was direct and individual. He felt the pope should be a shepherd rather than an absolute dictator. The papacy of his time was in turmoil. Wycliffe saw this conflict as proof that the church structure was in need of cleansing judgment.

Wycliffe also opposed the notion that the bread and wine of Holy Communion were actually changed into Christ's body and blood. He held up the Bible as the absolute authority for the church on earth. His attack

on the church would have cost him his life if the English government had not protected him.

Wycliffe also worked with a group of Oxford scholars to translate the Bible into the language of the people. Because of this work, the Wycliffe Bible Translators selected his name to identify their group.

HUS

The movement that Wycliffe began in England expanded and met with greater success in Bohemia. A strong national group, led by John Hus, contributed greatly to this success, and the Gospel ultimately spread to much of Europe.

John Hus, a priest and an instructor at the University of Prague (today the capital of Czechoslovakia) freely circulated Wycliffe's teachings. Using the paintings on the walls of his church for object lessons, Hus pointed out the contrast between the pope and Christ. While Christ was pictured humbly, walking barefoot, the pope rode a horse. Christ was pictured as washing His disciples' feet, while the pope preferred having his feet kissed.

This action by Hus caused the local church leaders to excommunicate him. Eventually he was put on trial and condemned to death—being burned at the stake in the year 1415.

Hus died because he refused to recant his belief that the church should be instructed by the Bible alone. He contributed greatly to the intellectual heritage of the church through his writings, though his greatest contributions may have been the personal Christian encouragement he gave to others.

LUTHER

Martin Luther was a German priest who searched for peace with God. While studying the Bible he came to realize that righteousness was not something people possessed because of their good works, but it was given them by Christ. When he nailed the 95 theses to the door of the Castle Church in Wittenberg, Luther stirred up opposition that eventually led to his excommunication from the church.

Local rulers took action to save Luther's life, and he was able to spend the rest of his life writing, preaching, and teaching God's Word.

ZWINGLI

Ulrich Zwingli led an early reform movement in Switzerland. A priest in Zurich, Zwingli was influenced a great deal by Luther's writings. At times, though, he changed worship more drastically than Luther did. For example, Luther had retained symbols like candles, statues, music, and pictures, but Zwingli rejected these in an attempt to imitate the church described in the New Testament, as he saw it.

Luther and Zwingli debated their beliefs in Marburg, Germany, in 1529. They agreed on many things, but Luther refused Zwingli's hand of fellowship, because they disagreed over the question of how Christ was present in the Lord's Supper. Zwingli felt that the bread and wine only symbolized the body and blood of Christ; Luther insisted that Christ's true body and blood were really present.

CALVIN

John Calvin continued the ministry that Zwingli had begun. He greatly influenced the Reformation movements in the second half of the 16th century.

Calvin and Luther both recognized God's grace and His sovereignty, but Luther placed a greater emphasis on His grace, and Calvin stressed His sovereignty. The doctrine of predestination illustrates this. Calvin taught that the sovereign God has chosen to save some to glorify His grace, and has allowed others to be condemned in order to glorify His justice. Luther taught that God in His grace wants *all* to be saved, but some reject Him and are, therefore, damned; others, chosen by God from eternity, are saved through Christ **(Ephesians 1:3–14).** Human logic would conclude that predestination to salvation must have its opposite, predestination to damnation, but the ways of God defy the limits of our reason.

KNOX

John Knox, of Scotland, was strongly influenced by Calvin's teachings. The modern Presbyterian church can trace its roots to Knox. He believed that Protestants had the right, if not the duty, to resist the Roman church. Knox desired a strict Puritanism, dedicated to purifying church and society.

WESLEY

The modern Methodist church can trace its history back to John Wesley (1703–91), who separated from the church of England and developed a theology that stressed methodical purity of life. John Wesley and his brother Charles (who wrote more than 6,000 hymns) worked tirelessly to spread the Gospel, especially among the poor. They and their followers also did their best to improve social conditions.

REFORM

The church that Christ established on earth has always been subject to the human limitations of its members. Weak and sinful humans *will* disagree with one another from time to time. Satan *will* attack Christ wherever He is worshiped or served. At the same time, we have Christ's promise that **the gates of hell will not overcome** His holy Christian church **(Matthew 16:18),** but we have no guarantee against splintering and division of the visible church.

Until Christ returns, the church will always need reform. We praise God for the reformers whom God used to return the church to the clear teachings of the Bible. And we rejoice that whenever people proclaim God's Word, it will accomplish the purpose for which He sent it: to turn sinners to the comforting and forgiving love of Christ.

REMEMBER

[As rain and snow cause the earth to yield seeds and bread,]*so is My word that goes out from My mouth: it will not return to Me empty, but will accomplish what I desire and achieve the purpose for which I sent it.*

Isaiah 55:11

FOR NEXT TIME

List significant events from Luther's life. What do you think makes Lutherans unique?

Session 12

Denominations: Let's Talk About It

[Jesus said,] "I pray also for those who will believe in Me through their message, that all of them may be one, Father, just as You are in Me, and I am in You. May they also be in Us, so that the world may believe that You have sent Me."

John 17:20–21

There are many different kinds of Christians in the world today—Baptists, Presbyterians, Methodists, Catholics, and others—who, together with Lutherans, believe that Jesus suffered, died, and rose again to redeem us from our sins. We are all Christians. Yet there are some differences in teachings among these groups. Can you name some of the differences?

THE RIGHTEOUSNESS OF GOD

You probably know that, even though Martin Luther studied and taught the Bible, he spent years seeking peace with God but finding only terror, because he felt that God condemned him for his sins. Finally, though, Luther realized that, yes, God does condemn sinners, but He also loves them and sent His Son, Jesus Christ, to save them from a life of fear and worry. Luther had never heard that preached or taught before, and he became very excited. The students in his classroom and the people below his pulpit began to hear of a very loving and gracious God who promised pardon for their sins.

The church of that day taught that people could get right with God by their contributions (through indulgences) or by good works. Luther contradicted that teaching. He had tried that approach—and failed. But then he discovered that the righteousness spoken of in the Bible was nothing that people could earn, but was something that God freely gives to anyone who believes in Him.

Bible verses like **Psalm 31:1** showed Luther the *comfort* of God's righteousness. Formerly he had dreaded God's presence, but now he welcomed it. For Christ's sake, God had declared Luther and other believers *righteous,* and **"the righteous will live by faith" (Romans 1:17).**Luther discovered that the righteousness of people like Abraham did not originate in themselves, but in God. **"Abraham believed God, and**

it was credited to him as righteousness" (Romans 4:3).

SCRIPTURE ALONE

Luther and others after him held up three banners for the world to see. These three watchwords—Scripture alone, grace alone, faith alone—were and are extremely important when talking about faith in God.

The Bible had dwindled in importance for the Roman Catholic church of Luther's day. *Traditions* had become a way of explaining many issues in the church. (Once the church officially adopted a teaching, everyone had to accept it without question.) The pope had become the supreme spiritual authority on earth. He could, for example, authorize the sale of indulgences. Through them the church offered forgiveness for sins and relief from a certain amount of time which people were to spend in purgatory.

Luther challenged these teachings. He insisted that we must determine church doctrine from the Bible, and the Bible alone. The Bible is inspired by God and necessary for all teaching **(2 Timothy 3:16).** Whenever we depart from teachings of the Bible, error creeps in, Luther said. Comfort is snatched from people, and they are left to pay for their sins with an uncertain amount of good deeds. Such teachings also insult God, who has already paid for our sins with the blood of His Son, Jesus.

GRACE ALONE

The church of Luther's day had certainly succeeded in putting the fear of God into people's hearts. But it had taught *only* the fear of God, that people could get right with God by *doing* things. Luther's study of Scripture led him to concentrate on what *Christ has already done* to purchase forgiveness for all the times when we don't do the right things. While many were counting up their good deeds, Luther was counting on the merits of Jesus, whose redemption had paid the total price.

Like Abraham, Luther discovered that God's righteousness could also be "credited to him" **(Romans**

4:22–24). Good works are nothing to boast about. People are saved by God's grace, as a free gift **(Ephesians 2:8–9).**

All the teachings of the Lutheran church center on this one doctrine, that we are saved only by grace through faith in Jesus Christ. Baptism works because of God's actions, not ours. Holy Communion was instituted and is continued by our gracious Lord Jesus. All people, if they are to stand justified before God, do so solely by the grace of our Lord Jesus Christ.

FAITH ALONE

What is faith? Most people would at the least say that faith means *to believe.* That's good. Faith does mean to believe. But believe in what? In what do you believe? Do you believe that there is air in this room? Can you prove it? How about two plus two equals four? Do you believe that?

1. Read **Romans 3:21–31.** What do you learn there about faith?

2. What insights about faith do you get from **Galatians 3:1– 9?**

3. How is *trust* related to faith? Write a definition of faith. Be sure to include the concept of trust.

A CONFESSIONAL CHURCH

The word *confession* has many meanings. A person who does something wrong is encouraged to *confess* his or her sins.

But a confession can also be positive. If we believe something, we are encouraged to make a *confession* of faith **(Romans 10:9).** We do this when we *confess* our faith in the Triune God, by speaking together the words of the Apostles' or the Nicene Creed. We make a *confession* of faith when we answer someone who asks us, "What do you believe?" or when we correct someone who makes a false statement about faith in Jesus.

Drawing on the writings of early reformers, the Lutheran church has developed a series of *Confessions* on which it is united. Beginning with Luther, Lutherans have refused to recognize a unity without confessional agreement. The earliest documents contained in the Lutheran Confession (aside from the three ancient creeds) are Luther's Large and Small Catechisms. The Augsburg Confession demonstrates that Lutherans are orthodox Christians. A companion work, the Apology of the Augsburg Confession (not an apology in the popular sense of the word) is an apology in the sense of a defense of some points in the Augsburg Confession. The Formula of Concord was completed in 1577, in an attempt to bring unity to the Lutheran Church in Germany after it had been disturbed by a number of controversies after Luther's death in 1546. Shorter documents by Luther and his co-worker Philipp Melanchthon complete the Lutheran Confessions, which are contained in a book simply called *The Book of Concord,* which appeared officially in 1580.

LET'S TALK ABOUT IT!

We have seen how the Lutheran Church arrived at its Confessions. It is clear then that it would not be willing to compromise any of these teachings, since they are all based on the Word of God. On the other hand, it is also clear that we should willingly discuss aspects of faith and life with other believers, inviting them to join in confessional unity with us. In keeping with the will of our Savior, Jesus Christ, we seek the unity He desired for His followers **(John 17:20–21).**

REMEMBER

As we have opportunity, let us do good to all people, especially to those who belong to the family of believers.

Galatians 6:10

Session 13

Denominations: Agreeing to Disagree

[Jesus said,] "My prayer is not for them alone. I pray also for those who will believe in Me through their message, that all of them may be one, Father, just as You are in Me and I am in You. May they also be in Us so that the world may believe that You have sent Me."

John 17:20–21

Dear friends, do not believe every spirit, but test the spirits to see whether they are from God, because many false prophets have gone out into the world.

1 John 4:1

THE MORE WE GET TOGETHER, THE HAPPIER WE'LL BE!

What do you think? Is bigger better? Would you rather go to a bigger school? Do you prefer a larger class in school? a larger church? Do you think big cars are the best, the safest?

It has become "the American way" to think that bigger is better. Look at our cities, the cars we drive, and the businesses we spawn. Perhaps it's a natural extension of the progress of the industrial revolution, but churches seem to be following suit.

Certainly there's nothing wrong with a church being big. The accounts describing the growth of the early church to 3,000 **(Acts 2:41)** and to 5,000 men **(4:4)** appear in a context of rejoicing. Problems arise, though, when the desire for more (a bigger church) comes primarily at the expense of the Gospel.

UNITED CHURCH OF CHRIST

The United Church of Christ was formed in 1957 by the merger of two diverse groups, the Congregational Christian Churches and the Evangelical and Reformed Church. Both merging denominations were already the results of previous mergers.

The General Council of the Congregational and Christian Churches was formed in 1931 from an earlier group also known as Congregationalist and a group known as "Christian Churches." These groups empha-

sized the sovereignty of the congregation and had no effective oversight of doctrine. The only test for membership in the "Christian Churches" was "Christian character."

The Evangelical and Reformed Church was formed in 1934 by a merger of the Evangelical Synod and the Reformed Church. The Evangelical Synod itself was a fusion of Lutheran and Reformed groups in Germany in the so-called Prussian Union of 1817. The Reformed Church, also with German roots, grew from an attempt to combine Lutheran and Calvinist elements while avoiding "extremes" of both groups and, therefore, placed little importance on confessional agreement.

These very diverse groups adopted the following Statement of Faith:

We believe in God, the Eternal Spirit, Father of our Lord Jesus Christ and our Father, and to his deeds we testify:

He calls the worlds into being, creates man in his own image and sets before him the ways of life and death.

He seeks in holy love to save all people from aimlessness and sin.

He judges men and nations by his righteous will declared through prophets and apostles.

In Jesus Christ, the man of Nazareth, our crucified and risen Lord, he has come to us and shared our common lot, conquering sin and death and reconciling the world to himself.

He bestows upon us his Holy Spirit, creating and renewing the Church of Jesus Christ, binding in covenant faithful people of all ages, tongues, and races.

He calls us into his Church to accept the cost and joy of discipleship, to be his servants in the service of men, to proclaim the gospel to all the world and resist the powers of evil, to share in Christ's baptism and eat at his table, to join him in his passion and victory.

He promises to all who trust him forgiveness of sins and fullness of grace, courage in the struggle for justice and peace, his presence in trial and rejoicing, and eternal life in his kingdom which has no end.

Blessing and honor, glory and power be unto him. Amen.

(Quoted from *The United Church of Christ,* by Douglas Horton [Thomas Nelson & Sons, 1962].)

This statement was adopted as "a testimony rather than a test of faith," and is not binding on anyone.

1. Compare the statement above with Luther's definitions of the First, Second, and Third Articles of the Apostles' Creed as written in The Small Catechism. What similarities do you find? What differences?

2. Compare the statement above with the following statements from The Augsburg Confession (reprinted from *The Book of Concord,* Muhlenberg Press, 1959):

- "There is one divine essence, which is called and which is truly God, and . . . there are three persons in this one divine essence . . . " (Article I).
- "Since the fall of Adam all men who are born according to the course of nature are conceived and born in sin . . ." (Article II).
- "God the Son became man, born of the virgin Mary, and . . . two natures, divine and human, are so inseparably united in one Person that there is one Christ, true God and true man, who was truly born, suffered, was crucified, died, and was buried . . . " (Article III).
- "We receive forgiveness of sin and become righteous before God by grace, for Christ's sake, through faith, when we believe . . . " (Article IV).
- "Baptism is necessary and . . . grace is offered through it. Children, too, should be baptized . . . " (Article IX).
- "The true body and blood of Christ are really present in the Supper of our Lord under the form of bread and wine . . . " (Article X).

UNITED CHURCH OF CANADA

A similar union was formed in Canada in 1925, following a merger of the Canadian Methodist, Congregational, and some Presbyterian churches. The United Church of Canada adopted a statement of faith, actually Twenty Articles. These articles of faith (succeeded in 1940 by Twelve Articles) sought to strike a medium point, avoiding the errors they felt were on extremes of the theological spectrum—those who stress people too much and those who stress proper doctrine too much. Because each of the merging groups had a different form of church government, agreement was sought by aligning local groups of two or three congregations which seemed to satisfy everyone.

EVANGELICAL LUTHERAN CHURCH IN AMERICA

A large Lutheran merger took place during the 1980s. On Jan. 1, 1988, The American Lutheran Church, the Lutheran Church in America, and the Association of Evangelical Lutheran Churches merged into the Evangelical Lutheran Church in America.

1. Find information about the Evangelical Lutheran Church in America. Then debate this statement: *The Evangelical Lutheran Church in America is an example of a merger that resulted when participants agreed to disagree.*

2. Why could The Lutheran Church—Missouri Synod not become a part of this new Lutheran merger?

3. What has prevented a merger of The Lutheran Church—Missouri Synod with the Wisconsin Evangelical Lutheran Synod?

ONE OR MANY

1. On the basis of two Bible verses at the beginning of this session, develop a statement to describe the way you would want to approach church mergers.

2. What additional insights do you find in **Jeremiah 32:38–39; Matthew 7:15; 24:11; John 17:11; Romans 16:17–19; 1 Thessalonians 5:21–22; 2 Peter 2:1?**

REMEMBER

Watch out for those who cause divisions and put obstacles in your way that are contrary to the teaching you have learned. Keep away from them. . . . Be wise about what is good, and innocent about what is evil.

Romans 16:17, 19

FOR NEXT TIME

Do you know anything about churches that have tried to return to the pattern of church structure demonstrated by early Christians? Try to list several groups that, either in doctrine or life-style, seem intent upon going "back to the basics."

Session 14

Iconoclasm: Back to Basics?

"IN THE BEGINNING THEY WERE ALL TOGETHER"

They devoted themselves to the apostles' teaching and to the fellowship .... All the believers were together and had everything in common.... Every day they continued to meet together in the temple courts.

Acts 2:42, 44, 46

1. Write two or three paragraphs describing the "togetherness" that you think existed in the Christian church of the New Testament (**Acts** through **Revelation**).

2. How does each of the following verses either support or dispute your opinion?

Acts 15:37–40
1 Corinthians 1:10–12
Galatians 1:6–7
Revelation 2:6, 15

IDEALIZING, OR IDOLIZING, "THE SIMPLE"

Life on the rugged American frontier of the early 1800s was a matter of survival, not of luxuries. The need to seek the essentials—the "basics"—extended to education and other areas of life, including religion. Far-flung neighbors of varying ethnic, cultural, and religious backgrounds would gather for church, often seeking a worship style that reflected their basic lifestyles. They might discard traditions, practices, liturgies, or doctrines of one particular denomination in order to find some basis for unity. Thus the soil of the American frontier was ripe for the growth of antidenominationalism.

KARLSTADT, THE FIRST SIMPLE LUTHERAN

Some of the roots of this movement developed while Martin Luther hid out at Wartburg Castle. At that time leadership of the Reformation fell into the hands of his fellow professor Andreas Karlstadt. Because he had strongly defended Luther in the first debates, Karlstadt was trusted by the early Lutherans.

With Luther in exile, Karlstadt tried to become "more Lutheran" than Luther. He added to Luther's own Biblical teachings some of the Old Testaments laws against pictures, images (*icons*), statues, and even church music. Soon some of the common people went on a rampage through the churches, destroying artwork, smashing stained-glass windows, and stripping the pastors of their churchly robes.

Karlstadt preached that all these external symbols were not needed; he eventually discarded even the sacraments of Baptism and the Lord's Supper. In their place he taught that Christians could find the pure spirit of Christ inside themselves and must show it by holy living. In this way "saints" could purify society, and eventually each man, woman, youth, and child would become so purely Christian that pastors and church teachers would no longer be necessary. Karlstadt became one of the earliest Protestant *iconoclasts*.

The civil unrest and riots caused by Karlstadt's preaching eventually forced the other Lutheran leaders to plead for Luther's return to Wittenberg. When Luther arrived, Karlstadt refused to back down from his radical position and finally, with sorrow "greater than I have known since my battle with Rome," Luther ordered Karlstadt to leave Wittenberg. Later, Luther wrote why Karlstadt's teachings could not be tolerated:

"I approached the task of destroying images by first tearing them out of the heart through God's Word.... For when they are no longer in the heart, they can do no harm when seen with the eyes. But Dr. Karlstadt ... has reversed the order by removing them from sight and leaving them in the heart! ...

"He blames me for protecting images ... though he knows that I seek to tear them out of the hearts of all.... It is only that I do not approve of his wanton violence and impetuosity.... He ... only smashes them in pieces outwardly, while he permits idols to remain in the heart and sets up others alongside them, namely false confidence and pride in works" (from "Against the Heavenly Prophets," *Luther's Works*, vol. 40, [Concordia, 1958], pages 84–85. Used by permission of Concordia Publishing House).

Luther feared that after people discarded images, customs, church music, and traditions, they would fill the vacuum with something worse: *false pride in one's own goodness.* He believed that if pictures, music, liturgical worship, robes, images, or stained-glass windows sent messages that did not contradict the Bible, they should be retained, not discarded. He saw that radicals who tried to discard such helps usually felt spiritually superior to struggling Christians.

Luther charged Karlstadt and the iconoclasts with forcing an outward "holiness" on people to make them seem pious. Luther insisted on retaining Christian freedom, on not forcing such laws and works on the Christian conscience. In a sarcastic moment Luther wrote that since Karlstadt and his fellow radicals claimed to possess the greatest inward spirituality of all Christians, then they must have "devoured the Holy Spirit, feathers and all!"

THE AMERICAN ICONOCLASTS

The American frontier preachers had no direct connection with Andreas Karlstadt, but the rugged environment and the geographical separation from established churches made fertile fields for America's own version of iconoclasm.

The Moravians

Originally formed as a movement to work as good leaven within the national church of Germany, the Moravians believed that a godly life was essential as evidence of saving faith and that it had greater importance than creeds. Early Moravian leaders, such as Christian David and Count von Zinzendorf, had little regard for doctrinal matters and, with missionary zeal, tried to create little "churches," or retreats away from worldly influences, within the large congregations in the European church bodies, in order to foster personal spirituality. Arriving in the United States in the early 18th century, the Moravians eventually gave up their hope of setting a "pure church" example to other Christians, and they became a denomination. Their work influenced later iconoclastic movements in North America.

The Campbellites

Thomas Campbell, son of a Scottish Presbyterian, despised denominational churches and teachings. He and his son Alexander preached throughout the frontier that non-Biblical terms (such as Lutheran) should be discarded, and that creeds, liturgical worship, confessional statements, and church structure should be discarded, because they were barriers to Christian unity.

The Campbellites probably would have faded from the American scene had Alexander Campbell not joined with Barton Stone to form the denomination known as the Disciples of Christ.

Disciples of Christ

Alexander Campbell's followers preferred to be called "Disciples," while Stone's followers chose "Christian." In 1832 the Christians and Disciples joined to form the denomination known today as the Christian Church (Disciples of Christ). They adopted the term Restoration to refer to their movement to restore what they believed were the patterns and practices of the New Testament.

As a denomination that believes creeds to be divisive, we can compare the Christian Church (Disciples of Christ) to an umbrella that covers a variety of teachings and practices. One can expect, therefore, to find totally divergent views among the leaders of the Disciples. Holding to the idea that personal Christian liberty may allow different views, the Disciples do not agree, for instance, on the virgin birth of Christ Jesus or the inspiration (and inerrancy) of the Scriptures.

In spite of this noncreedal stance, Disciples tend to agree on some doctrines. They see conversion as a voluntary action of the individual, rather than due to the working of God through the Word. They have no method for instruction before membership. Any baptized Christian may be admitted to the Lord's Supper, since they regard it as symbolic. They downplay doctrinal theology, but see right living as important—important enough that right living has become, for Disciples, the basis of church fellowship.

In summary, we find no historical or cultural connection between the Disciples of Christ and Andreas Karlstadt, but the similarities of their teachings are remarkably close. Both viewed Biblical doctrines and practice as divisive and, as a result, lost the opportunity to unite around Scripture with other Christians. Attempting to be a movement to unite all denominations, they became yet another denomination.

REMEMBER

Jesus said, "If you hold to My teaching, you are really My disciples. Then you will know the truth, and the truth will set you free."

John 8:31–32

FOR NEXT TIME

Look up the word *Calvinism* in a Bible dictionary. See what you can learn about the theological concept that bears John Calvin's name.

Session 15

Movements in Protestantism: Calvinism

WHY WAS THE BIBLE WRITTEN?

I write these things to you who believe in the name of the Son of God, so that you may know that you have eternal life.

1 John 5:13

ZWINGLI: THE RADICAL REFORMER

You were introduced to Ulrich Zwingli when you studied the Reformation in session 11. You may recall that Zwingli wanted to throw out everything that reminded people of the Roman Catholic church. Actually, he wanted to reform worship more than doctrine. He had seen people flock into the small town in which he was pastor. These people were accustomed to paying to view relics (alleged remains of the Virgin Mary and other saints). Zwingli said that God didn't work with people through any external means. He said that the Holy Spirit didn't need any vehicle.

Zwingli not only opposed the teachings of the Catholic church. He worked and *fought* to have laws enacted that would outlaw actions such as the viewing of relics as a public nuisance and an abomination to God. He died on the battlefield, serving as chaplain in a war to defend his reforms.

CALVIN: A THEOLOGICAL GIANT

You met John Calvin in session 11. He is still considered one of the greatest systematic thinkers of all time. At the age of 27 he finished his famous and extensive *Institutes of the Christian Religion*. This monumental work in systematic theology established Calvin as a prominent theological figure.

Calvin set about to reform whatever needed reforming. He gained control of the city government of Geneva, Switzerland, and helped pass laws that would regulate every aspect of life in the community.

Calvin believed that the Bible was the precise expression of God's will. Since God was sovereign in all areas of human activity, it was unthinkable to say that people who went to hell did so against the will of

God. If God was supreme and sovereign, Calvin reasoned, this too must be part of God's will. This led to the doctrine of double predestination. Calvin said that God had saved some to glorify His grace, and damned others (unbelievers) to glorify His justice.

Review what you learned about predestination in session 11. See especially **Ephesians 1:11** and **Romans 8:28–30**. Also recall the comfort that God wants you to know in Jesus. See, for example, **John 10:27–28**.

INFLUENCE ON THE MODERN PRESBYTERIAN CHURCH

No church follows the teachings of Calvin entirely. However, we see the influence of Calvinism on the modern Presbyterian church, especially in the area of predestination. One part of the Westminster Confession (a Presbyterian statement of beliefs) states that by the decree of God, for the manifestation of His glory, some men and angels are predestined to everlasting life, and others are foreordained to everlasting death.

COMMON AND SPECIAL GRACE

Calvin said that not all people were included in God's plan of salvation. While all are recipients of God's "common" grace, which allows them to worship and serve God on a natural level, only those chosen by Him receive His "special" grace and are saved.

PRESBYTERIAN FORM OF CHURCH GOVERNMENT

The Bible spoke of "elders" or "presbyters." Calvin favored the presbyterian form of church government, in which presbyters, elected by the people, ruled the churches. This form of church government was vastly different from the papacy of Rome, which had a hierarchical governing structure.

The members of local congregations had the ability to express their wishes by voting for presbyters themselves. Their leaders were closer to them and, therefore, more approachable. Individual congregations were still not independent, however, since the presbyters met jointly to make decisions that would affect all the churches under their jurisdiction.

CALVINISM AND BAPTISM

Both Calvin and Luther recognized two sacraments, Baptism and Holy Communion. But they disagreed over the meaning of these sacraments. The Calvinistic (or Reformed) emphasis is on "symbolic parallels between the Old and New Testament actions of God."

Calvin drew rather extensive parallels between the rites of circumcision and Baptism and between the Passover and Holy Communion.

Calvin said that a child born into a Christian family is automatically a part of God's family. Calvinists stress the action of the community in bringing the child for baptism; Lutherans stress the act of God, who works through the means He has provided. Lutherans speak of forgiveness and regeneration (rebirth) through Holy Baptism; Calvinists speak only of a symbolism in the act of Baptism.

CALVINISM AND HOLY COMMUNION

Luther taught the Real Presence of Christ in Holy Communion (that is, the *true* body and blood of Christ are *really* present), but Zwingli, and later Calvin, disagreed. It was impossible, they reasoned, for Christ to be physically present in several places at once.

Calvinists do speak of Christ's "spiritual" presence, but then place emphasis on the obedience of the Christian rather than on the gracious invitation of Christ. Calvinism does not teach that Christ gives forgiveness and the assurance of eternal life as we receive the bread and wine. Calvinist churches emphasize Christ's command, **"Do this in remembrance of Me"** (1 Corinthians 11:24–25). Lutherans, on the other hand, emphasize the words of Christ, **"This is My body . . . this is My blood"** (1 Corinthians 11:24, Matthew 26:28).

COMFORT FROM CHRIST, FOR CHRIST'S

In, with, and under the bread and wine Christ gives us His true body and blood for the forgiveness of all our sins. As we eat and drink, we receive the comfort that Christ wants us to have. Similarly, in Baptism we receive the blessings of Christ's death **(Romans 6:4)**.

By emphasizing God's grace, rather than His sovereignty, we receive complete comfort and the positive assurance: **"While we were still sinners, Christ died for us" (Romans 5:8)**. He rose again, so that we can know for sure that we have eternal life. This is why the Bible was written in the first place. This is real comfort, coming from Christ, for us, His own children. Rejoice in it, and live for Him!

REMEMBER

Since we have been justified through faith, we have peace with God through our Lord Jesus Christ, through whom we have gained access by faith into this grace in which we now stand. And we rejoice in the hope of the glory of God.

Romans 5:1–2

FOR NEXT TIME

Look up *Arminianism* in a theological dictionary or encyclopedia. See what you can learn about this religious movement. Can you discover the time period during which this movement began, and when it was strongest? Among which groups is it strongest today? Why?

Session 16

Movements in Protestantism Arminianism

GOD BROUGHT YOU TO LIFE TWICE

As for you, you were dead in your transgressions and sins, in which you used to live when you followed the ways of this world . . . . But because of His great love for us, God, who is rich in mercy, made us alive with Christ even when we were dead in transgressions—it is by grace you have been saved.

Ephesians 2:1–2, 4–5

Have you ever heard about someone who, after being very close to death told about a "near-death" experience? Typically these people felt as if they were leaving their bodies, and in many cases were able to watch doctors and nurses working frantically to save them. They traveled down a long, dark tunnel, attracted irresistibly by a brilliant light at the other end. When they finally reached the light, some have told of meeting Jesus and receiving instructions to return to their body and lives and "try harder" to do His will.

Medical people may be skeptical, but such experiences are being related with increasing frequency. These people have obviously had some kind of experience, one that moves them to view their "new life" as a second chance.

Consider, however, that we all *have* been given another chance—by God (and more—God has given us the *certainty* of salvation). We were all created by Him but, because of sin, we were all once dead in our sins and trespasses. But God **made us alive** again. In Christ He graciously gave us new life. God again made us His sons and daughters and empowered us to live to His glory.

One movement within Christendom, Arminianism, places the emphasis on us and our ability to make decisions and to do things that please God.

JACOB ARMINIUS

A Dutch theologian, Jacob Arminius (1560–1609), objected to the Calvinistic doctrine of God's uncondi-

tional double predestination. He felt that this limited Christ's atonement and actually made God the author of sin. Followers of Arminius, called Arminians, followed Zwingli and Calvin in their teaching on the sacraments and other matters, but on predestination and related matters they tended to focus attention off of God and onto humanity. Arminius and his followers stressed human ability, free will, good deeds, and feelings.

We find Arminian theology today in varying degrees in the Methodists, the Holiness groups, and the Salvation Army. John Wesley (1703–91) helped popularize Arminian theology.

JOHN AND CHARLES WESLEY

The Methodist church owes its beginnings largely to the workings of John Wesley. Wesley is often considered the third great Protestant leader, after Luther and Calvin.

Wesley's movement began as a reaction against the Church of England, because of its coldness and formalism and because it tolerated many extreme viewpoints. Queen Elizabeth I, among others, had hoped that Christians of many different persuasions could coexist in one Christian church. Later the Puritans had tried and generally failed to *purify* the church from within.

Still later, deism and rationalism had crept into the church and seriously undermined its integrity. Deism sought to reduce God to an impersonal "Supreme Being." Rationalism rejected anything that couldn't be understood by reason. The church gradually became the playground of the rich and privileged and offered little for the poor and underprivileged.

Pietism had already emerged within Lutheranism to combat the rationalistic direction of many scholars. The Church of England was ripe for a similar movement when John Wesley and his brother Charles appeared on the scene. Appalled by the worldliness of their fellow students at Oxford University, the Wesley brothers formed what jeering fellow students called the "Holy Club," whose members were called "Methodists." The

Wesleys were pursuing especially the attainment of holiness or perfection through methodical observance of rules and regulations. They were concerned more with life-style than with doctrines.

THE METHODIST CHURCH

John Wesley himself described a Methodist as "one who lives according to the method laid down in the Bible; who loves the Lord with all his heart and prays without ceasing; whose heart is full of love toward all mankind and is purified from envy, malice, wrath and every unkind affection; who keeps all God's commandments from the least unto the greatest; who follows not the customs of the world; who cannot speak evil of his neighbor any more than he can lie; who does good to all men. . . . These are the marks of a Methodist. By these alone the Methodists desire to be distinguished from other men" (*The Christian Advocate,* May 19, 1938).

Methodists today are divided into about 20 groups. Most Methodists in the United States are part of The United Methodist Church, which was established in 1968 as the result of several mergers.

HOLINESS GROUPS

The Wesleyan movement arose largely as a reaction against the Church of England's coldness and formalism. However, as the Methodist Church itself became a larger, established church, it too became somewhat formal and lost much of its original militant, crusading spirit.

Some Methodists were very unhappy with this. These people demanded complete holiness of life, making it their main doctrinal concern. When the Methodist Church did not make holines a priority concern, the protesters formed their own body.

The largest of these Holiness groups is the Church of the Nazarene. It teaches that after we receive faith in the Lord Jesus, we are sanctified wholly, and that the Holy Spirit bears witness to the new birth and also to the entire sanctification of believers.

Holiness groups believe that the Holy Spirit baptizes individuals, and they become "born again." They then are instantly transformed into a state of "complete sanctification," where they can no longer commit a willful sin. Holiness groups include the Church of God and The Christian and Missionary Alliance.

PENTECOSTAL GROUPS

Other Arminians, the "Pentecostal" churches, generally regard the "baptism in the Holy Spirit" to be far more important and effective than the water baptism instituted by Christ.

They speak of a "full Gospel," which they say is "Foursquare." It refers to four parts, Christ the Savior, Sanctifier, Healer, and Coming King. In looking at His coming kingship, they emphasize a literal 1,000-year reign on earth by Christ with His followers.

Many of these churches include "Pentecostal" in their name, although the Assemblies of God and Churches of God are also Pentecostal.

In recent years, Pentecostals, or "charismatics," as they are often called, have made inroads into almost every major denomination, including Catholic, Lutheran, Baptist, and Episcopalian. Sometimes called Neo-Pentecostal, these people have expressed an interest in revitalizing their churches.

THE SALVATION ARMY

While not considered a church by many, the Salvation Army, has all the marks of a church, including organization, worship services, and administrative structures. It follows many of the principles chosen by the Wesleys for their "method." Primarily an organization for social service, its central theme is also holiness of life.

PROBLEMS WITH ARMINIANISM

Since Arminianism emphasizes the native abilities of people, rather than the grace of God, its followers, if they pursue their error to the end, deny salvation by grace alone and, at least to a small degree, trust in themselves for salvation.

It is important to stress that Christ alone has saved us. We err when we emphasize our own native abilities or our emotions. Look rather to Christ, **"the author and perfecter of our faith" (Hebrews 12:2).**

REMEMBER

You were washed, you were sanctified, you were justified in the name of the Lord Jesus Christ and by the Spirit of our God.

1 Corinthians 6:11

FOR NEXT TIME

Look up the word *synergism* in both a regular and a theological dictionary. How does *synergism* differ from Arminianism?

Session 17

Movements in Protestantism: Synergism

WHAT WOULD YOU SAY?

Imagine sitting in a waiting room somewhere, with time on your hands. You strike up a conversation with a lady sitting next to you and discover that she does not believe she is going to heaven. What would you do and say so that by the time you leave she would know the way to heaven? Take a sheet of paper and briefly outline what you would say. Note which Scriptures you would quote, if any. Try to anticipate the arguments you might get in response to your statements.

WHAT MUST I DO TO BE SAVED?

"Sirs, what must I do to be saved?" . . . "Believe in the Lord Jesus, and you will be saved" (Acts 16:30–31).

WHAT IS SYNERGISM?

One dictionary defines *synergism* as "the joint action of agents, as drugs, that when taken together increase each other's effectiveness." Strictly speaking, *synergistic* means "working together."

In theology we define *synergism* as "the idea that people can cooperate in their conversion." We find many similarities between synergism and Arminianism.

One of Martin Luther's best friends and fellow workers in the Reformation, Philipp Melanchthon, advanced the idea of synergism (primarily after Luther's death). Melanchthon reasoned that if a person is saved, it is caused by three forces *working together*: God's Word, the Holy Spirit, and man's will not resisting God's Word. Many scholars since have said this is where Melanchthon got himself into trouble; He *reasoned*.

Erasmus, the Dutch scholar who had provided Luther with the Greek text of the Bible, had said many of the same things. He taught that people, at the very least, had the ability to take God's grace into themselves, thus limiting the Biblical concept of salvation by grace alone.

IS IT SCRIPTURAL?

While the Formula of Concord thoroughly repudiated the idea of synergism, the damage had been done. Lutheranism had been exposed to the infectious disease of synergism, and periodic interest has been expressed in the *logical* error of synergism. The Formula of Concord clearly states that we cannot save ourselves. In our salvation we are passive, not active!

Read **Ephesians 2:8–10** and **Romans 3:23–28**. Now go back to the exercise we did at the beginning of class. If you are going to be one of God's useful tools in converting this lady to faith in Jesus Christ, you must remember that she can be saved only by God's grace. Did you try to convert her by yourself? Did you try to convince her of the rightness of Christianity?

Both of these are synergistic errors that suggest that people can save themselves. Though it may seem very logical, synergism disagrees with the teachings of the Bible.

What do you think would happen if you, after being schooled in the idea of *salvation by grace through faith*, began to believe that people could be converted by themselves? Would it damage your faith?

The evangelistic crusades and strong revival movements that swept the United States in the late 1800s and into the 1900s have conveyed strong pictures as to how people are saved. You may have a mental picture of large crowds of people, heads bowed, souls pricked, under the strong Law preaching of a revivalist-style preacher. Or perhaps you have seen a cartoon of a man carrying a sign saying, "Repent, for the end is at hand." He drops his sign, runs up and grabs a passerby by the collar, and attempts to browbeat him into believing. These strong images are reinforced by the televised crusades in which thousands of people record their decision for Christ by responding to an altar call.

All people since the fall into sin are born sinful and are spiritually dead—against God. Rescue—salvation—depends totally on God's grace and mercy.

But we can't simply leave it at that. We know that people are saved by grace. We must ourselves learn what Scripture says about the conversion of a sinner.

And then we must alert others to the dangers of Arminianism and synergism.

WHAT DOES SCRIPTURE TEACH ABOUT CONVERSION?

First of all, Scripture teaches that all who are born of sinful flesh inherit the sinfulness of their fleshly and sinful parents (**John 3:6**). All people have inherited that sinful condition (**Romans 5:12**), which results in death. All people are by nature spiritually blind (**2 Corinthians 4:4**), spiritually dead (**Ephesians 2:1, 5**), and actually God's enemies (**Romans 5:10**). Not only can't we *see* God and His will, we can't *move* toward Him, because we're dead. In fact, left to our own devices, we will move away from, and against God as fast as we can.

Second, God really **"wants all men to be saved and to come to a knowledge of the truth"** (**1 Timothy 2:4**). He wants no one to be damned in hell (**Ezekiel 33:11**). Christ came into the world to redeem it to Himself so everyone may be one with Him (**2 Corinthians 5:19**). If people *are not* saved, it is not the fault of God, but of the people themselves! And if they *are* saved, it is solely God's doing (*monergism*). While *synergism* suggests that people can *work together* with God, *monergism* stresses that it is God alone who works faith in people.

Problems arise when people use their minds to work out God's truth. Working from logic, and not from Scripture, we may conclude that if people can resist God's gracious invitation, we can also cooperate with Him and be saved.

CHRISTIANITY AND SYNERGISM

Let's examine several of the objections to *monergism*. The objections are printed in italics.

1. **Fatalism.** "*If people can do nothing about their salvation, they will become careless and fatalistic.*" What do **Matthew 10:29** and **John 10:28** say about fatalism and God?

2. **Mechanism.** "*If people are entirely passive, then conversion is mechanical.*" Read about how Jesus Himself called disciples, and note that while there is nothing mechanical about it, He also doesn't force them to do anything. He simply offers Himself to them (**Matthew 4:19, 21–22; 9:9**). He invites people to come to Him for saving and for comfort (**11:28**), but recognizes that many will reject His free and gracious offer (**23:37**).

3. **Cooperation.** "*If we have the power to reject Christ, then we must also have the power to accept Him.*" We are able to "accept" Christ only by the power of the Holy Spirit (**1 Corinthians 12:3**). Remember, it is God who made us and who re-made us after the fall into sin (**2 Corinthians 5:19**). People don't confess Him, because they reject His Spirit and the messengers He sends (**1 Corinthians 12:3; Luke 7:30; 13:34**). Since all people are by nature spiritually dead (**Ephesians 2:1, 5**), we cannot cooperate with God in our conversion.

4. **Less resistance.** "*Lightning follows the path of least resistance, and so does God. If people can resist God, then they must also have the power to cease resisting, or at least resist a little less! Those are the people God saves.*" The problems with *cooperation* also apply here.

SPEAK THE GOSPEL

Do you remember how Jesus approached people? He simply invited them. With His Spirit working, some followed Him, but others rejected Him and went away sad or angry. At all times Jesus was always ready to receive sinners to Himself.

Synergism certainly *sounds* logical, but it isn't Scriptural. Any time you have an opportunity to speak to someone about Jesus, be sure to do it. But be sure to point people to the comforting message of salvation, which Jesus has completed for us. Remember, you don't need to convince people to be saved; the Holy Spirit does that! God wants you to talk to them and, for the sake of Jesus, love them. Remember, He loves everyone and wants everyone to be saved!

REMEMBER

God, who said, "Let light shine out of darkness," made His light shine in our hearts to give us the light of the knowledge of the glory of God in the face of Christ.

2 Corinthians 4:6

Session 18

Review of Sessions 10–17

Give brief, yet complete, answers to the following questions.

1. What does *catholic* mean?

2. What does *orthodox* mean?

3. What event in 1054 forever changed the shape of Christianity?

4. To what event and person does the Roman Catholic church trace its origin?

5. List several similarities between the Lutheran and Roman Catholic churches.

6. List several differences between the Lutheran and Roman Catholic churches.

7. What event on Oct. 31, 1517, forever changed the course of Christianity?

8. List several reasons why John Wycliffe felt the need for a reformation of the church and mention significant things he did to promote it.

9. Describe the contribution John Hus made to the Protestant Reformation.

10. What circumstances allowed Luther to protest successfully against the Roman Catholic church?

11. To what was Luther objecting most when he posted his 95 theses?

12. What issue separated Luther and Zwingli?

13. Mention important contributions by Calvin, Knox, and Wesley as church reformers.

14. Why is the church in constant need of reform?

15. Name and describe the three "alones" ("solas") that have become mottoes of the Lutheran Reformation. Explain why each is important to a proper understanding of the Bible and salvation.

16. Describe how Luther came to object to the official teachings of the Roman Catholic Church.

17. Explain Luther's understanding of **Psalm 31:1; Romans 1:16;** and **Romans 4:3.**

18. Why is the Bible so important?

19. Why is the teaching of salvation by grace alone so important?

20. Describe the different understandings of faith, and describe the correct Biblical view of faith.

21. Explain *confessionalism.*

22. Why is it important to reach unity before declaring it?

23. Name two church groups that have formed new denominations by merging with other church groups.

24. While Jesus, in **John 17:20–21,** stressed the importance of unity within the body of Christ, explain why we find so much separation.

25. Define *iconoclasm.*

26. Explain the feelings of the Campbellites toward creeds.

27. Explain why the pattern of the Campbellites was especially attractive to people who settled the early American frontiers.

28. Who was John Calvin, and what is significant about his church leadership?

29. What is Calvin's teaching about double predestination?

30. Describe the theology of Jacob Arminius.

31. Explain the contributions of John and Charles Wesley in popularizing Arminianism.

32. Explain why Arminianism is dangerous to the Christian faith.

33. Describe how a Holiness church differs from a Lutheran church.

34. What is synergism?

35. Why is synergism dangerous?

36. Why can't you save anyone, and why is it that God alone can save people?

UNIT 4

The Established Cults

Have you ever heard someone talking about "a cult" and thought they said "occult"? There is a difference, you know. A "cult" is any religious group that differs in its teachings from the "main" body. For the purposes of study in this unit, the "main" body we will be talking about is historic Christianity. *Occultism,* on the other hand, is the study of the occult, of hidden knowledge, and often of Satanic practices, such as witchcraft, magic, and spiritist attempts to contact the dead. Although many non-Christian cultic leaders use *occult* practices, we will deal more thoroughly with the occult or satanic cults in Unit 6.

Non-Christian cults seem to flourish in the United States. American people seem to be joiners. We like to get involved in groups. We get excited about joining something. People living in the United States today are also more *accessible* than people anywhere else in the world. We have more reading material coming directly into our homes each day than any other culture in the world. We can be contacted directly by telephone, radio, and television. People can move about freely from place to place without attracting a lot of attention. Our country makes an excellent breeding ground for all sorts of organizations, including cults.

As you study cults, notice that various characteristics of people attract them to cults. Everyone has needs. You have the need to love and be loved. You have the need to be close to others at times and to be alone at other times. People have needs that often, for one reason or another, aren't being met by "mainline" churches.

As you study this unit, think about your membership in a Christian congregation. We will talk about the cults that have been around for awhile—the established cults. As you study, ask yourself, "How could my church have met the needs of people who became involved in this group?" Then ask the Lord to provide you with opportunities to witness your faith to a cult member. **"Always be prepared to give an answer to everyone who asks you to give the reason for the hope that you have. But do this with gentleness and respect"** (1 Peter **3:15).** Consider the joy of knowing that someone believes in the Lord because you shared the hope of heaven with him or her!

May God's peace be with you!

Session 19

Cults: What Are They?

ITCHING EARS

The time will come when men will not put up with sound doctrine. Instead, to suit their own desires, they will gather around them a great number of teachers to say what their itching ears want to hear. They will turn their ears away from the truth and turn aside to myths.

2 Timothy 4:3–4

TOO GOOD TO BE TRUE

"When you meet the friendliest people you have ever known, who introduce you to the most loving group of people you've ever encountered, and you find the leader to be the most inspired, caring, compassionate, and understanding person you've ever met, and then you learn that the cause of the group is something you never dared to hope could be accomplished, and all of this sounds too good to be true—it probably is too good to be true—don't give up your education, your hopes and ambitions to follow a rainbow" (Jeanne Milles, survivor of Jonestown, as quoted in a tract from *Free Minds,* Box 4213, Minneapolis, MN 55414). Have you ever discovered something that was "too good to be true"? Perhaps you thought at the time that you were dreaming. Many people who have been involved with cults return with similar stories. And many of them are thankful to have escaped alive!

WHAT IS A CULT?

Have you ever wondered why some people get involved in cults? Have you perhaps wondered what a cult is? Before we begin this lesson, think for a moment. What do you think a cult is? How would you define a cult?

Write your definition of a cult in your notebook. Then look the word up in several dictionaries.

WHY DO CULTS BEGIN?

Can you imagine why anyone would try to begin a new religion? Think back to the first few sessions. All religions help people to answer basic questions about life and existence. How many of those questions can you remember?

Most cults begin with one individual. This person may begin with a noble purpose, such as helping people. Sometimes, though, the person begins with the express purpose of fooling people and gaining popularity for himself. Usually he chooses one particular goal or theme, such as world peace or the elimination of problems between people. By logically extending this goal, the leader can make promises that seem very attractive. Often followers take this bait before they realize what is happening.

HOW DO CULTS BEGIN?

Cults have flourished in this country in the past 20 years for various reasons. Problems—such as hunger, unemployment, and threats of war and annihilation—persist, despite massive attempts to meet these challenges. An informational blitz is burying the world in knowledge while at the same time the world shrinks with improved and increased communications systems. The world almost seems to be threatened with self-destruction by ecological and nuclear problems. Uncertainty about jobs plagues some; others don't know what to do with ever-increasing amounts of leisure time. Many people feel a lack of "roots" because of the great mobility required by jobs, leisure, and technology.

In the midst of all these changes, some churches have become secularized, as belief in the supernatural loses popularity. Values once universally taught by the church are being questioned and changed. Also, there seems to be a great deal of emphasis on the "packaging" of religion for certain audiences. People of all ages are confused with what "church" is.

God in Christ has come to our world with an eternal message. Even though we may change and times may change, God never changes. We always have the same need to receive forgiveness and the same assurance of salvation. But we must constantly be on our guard. Just being educated doesn't make us immune to the lure of cults. As children of the King—Jesus—we must stay close to Him. We do that by staying in

His Word, listening to His Words, remembering our baptism, receiving Communion, and offering our words to Him in prayer.

HOW SHOULD WE REACT TO CULTS?

Perhaps you have heard someone say, "I won't argue about politics or religion." Many have decided this after getting "burned" in an argument that no one could win. Or perhaps when asked about their religion, you have heard someone say, "That's too personal. I don't want to talk about it." Perhaps you should decide how you will witness to people. What will you say if they don't want to talk to you?

Also plan your reaction if someone from a cult approaches you. What will you do? What will you say?

First of all, agree to talk only about worthwhile things **(Philippians 4:8).** Don't get caught in the trap of running other religions down. With Paul, decide that when you talk to others about religion, your conversation will center on Jesus Christ and what He has done for all people **(1 Corinthians 2:2).** Be careful not to become sidetracked on some other issue, which is exactly what a cult member wants.

If you are going to find out anything about a cult member, find out what he or she thinks of Jesus **(Matthew 16:13–19).** When you talk about religion, show Jesus in all His glory and simplicity. Quote a simple Bible verse, like **John 3:16,** and share what it means to you to know that, because of Jesus' death and resurrection, you have eternal life as a free gift. Whenever you have the opportunity to respond to a cult, may God bless you!

REMEMBER

When they arrest you, do not worry about what to say or how to say it. At that time you will be given what to say, for it will not be you speaking, but the Spirit of your Father speaking through you.
Matthew 10:19–20

FOR NEXT TIME

Look up the meaning of the word *heresy.* List some false teachings that have arisen in the church.

Session 20

Cults: What Do They Offer?

TEST THE SPIRITS

Two boys are talking before school. The first boy says to the second boy: "What's the difference between a potato and a rock?" Suspecting a trick, the second boy replies: "I don't know." The first boy continues: "I wouldn't send *you* to the store for potatoes." And then he laughed!

Obviously the second boy knew the difference, but he also suspected a trick. People suspect tricks when it comes to religion, too. They wonder about the differences between religions. Many genuinely want to be able to identify false religions. But what about the tricky ones?

In the last session, we looked at cults—what they are and how they lead people astray. Many cults aren't really new. They simply pick up and continue a false doctrine that has existed for centuries. But how do you identify a cult, or any false religion? Listen to what the Bible says.

"Dear friends, do not believe every spirit, but test the spirits to see whether they are from God, because many false prophets have gone out into the world. This is how you can recognize the Spirit of God: Every spirit that acknowledges that Jesus Christ has come in the flesh is from God, but every spirit that does not acknowledge Jesus is not from God" (1 John 4:1–3).

In order to "test the spirits," we must know what we believe. Then look at other religions. Pay particular attention to what they say about Jesus Christ. Look beyond the questions of whether a real flesh-and-blood person name Jesus ever lived. Ask whether they believe that Jesus came into the flesh to die for the sins of the world.

CULTS OFFER NEWNESS
New Teaching

Many people are itching to hear something new. Cults thrive on these desires. Their leaders may offer new teachings, a new life-style, a new identity, new freedoms, or a new source of authority to replace "the old, old story of Jesus and His love." Can you give examples to illustrate how cults appeal to this desire for "newness"?

New Leaders

Almost all religious cults are built around a strong central person, usually the founder. Often this is a strong, dynamic leader, who projects the image of a father-figure. Quite often the leader claims to be God, or at least the Messiah. As the "only source of *true* wisdom," these strong leaders are often able to convince some to follow them blindly.

Strong cultic leaders often describe the rest of the world as bad, and invite recruits into a paradise that promises relief from all its problems. This attracts many—and not only young people.

New Life-Styles

Cults often attract young people by appealing to their natural needs. Young people who are fed up with parental supervision may jump at the chance to be "really free"—and that's what they perceive that cultic leaders are offering them.

A cultic leader often separates his flock from the rest of the world by removing them physically, or at least cutting off all information from the outside. Leaders like this often set up a strict hierarchy, with themselves at the top. They claim to have the only true authority. This new master may make promises to recruits and even deliver on them—until the trap is sprung and it's too late.

You can often identify a cult by the strict controls imposed on members. They are often deprived of sleep, nourishing food, and leisure time. After a while under such treatment, cult members tend to be quite suggestible.

One young cult dropout admitted joining a very idealistic group and being very impressed with its ideals. Not until this person had been with the group for some 10 days and had made a long-term commitment did he hear the name of the main leader—and express disappointment. "But, by that time, it was too late. I was hooked!" he said.

CULTS OFFER IMMEDIATE ANSWERS

We usually don't like to wait for answers to our questions. Many cult leaders capitalize on our impatience. Often through a brief conversation with someone, they can discover the key that will unlock that person's defenses.

Some young people are very idealistic. They become disillusioned with the world as they perceive it. They may feel that the answers and solutions offered by their parents and teachers are inadequate. Cultic leaders exploit this idealism. They offer answers for hunger, joblessness, etc. Unfortunately, their answers are almost always empty and entirely deceptive.

Have you ever prayed for a particular need and been frustrated that God didn't answer your prayer just as you would have liked? Can you see how we could get into trouble by believing that someone has all the answers? Have you ever bought a product advertised as the "be-all and end-all," only to discover that it wasn't? Have you ever discovered, too late, that you needed to spend a lot of additional money to make a certain product work properly? Cults are like that. Their promises may sound good until you have invested so much of yourself emotionally that it is too late to back out.

CULTS OFFER SOMETHING FALSE OR FAKE

False Teachings

Go back to the Scripture printed at the beginning of this lesson. You can always test the spirit of a particular religion by asking what it teaches about Jesus Christ. All cults somehow distort the doctrine of our Savior. See how many of these distortions you already know.

False Promises

Invariably, cults also make promises. To the lonely they offer companionship. To the poor they may offer money. To the sick or suffering they offer healing. Many recruits to cults have serious adolescent adjustment problems, but many others seem well adjusted. Regardless of which group a recruit is from, cult recruiters skillfully discover an unmet need and promise satisfaction.

Young people often perceive that their church lays guilt on them. Cults often attract new members by promising relief from that guilt, simply by joining. To some this appears to be *grace*, much like true Christianity. Nothing could be farther from the truth. Only a false religion offers forgiveness that is not based on the shed blood of Jesus Christ!

CULTS MAKE REQUIREMENTS TOO!

Once the "bait" is taken, recruits discover that cults make requirements of them too! Cults always require a certain amount of *sacrifice*, like interrupting an education or career and giving up family. They may even misapply Scripture to back up their claims **(Matthew 10:35–39).** Cults require an investment, usually of time and money. As the relationship with the cult grows, so does the investment, until it is complete! Very jealous of other relationships, cults invariably require a renunciation of all past relationships, including family and friends.

A recruit who has renounced former relationships has no choice but to establish a close communion with the new group. Cults teach that the group is more important than the individual. This is called *transcendence.* The importance of the individual is lost in the multitude. Then cults can justify a denial of self, including pleasures, and ultimately even bodily needs.

FIGHT FIRE WITH FIRE!

To deal with a cult we must confront the issues head on. Instead of arguing, politely listen to what cult members have to say, and then ask for the same courtesy of them. Center your comments on what the Bible clearly says about Jesus Christ, and His blood-bought forgiveness for your sins. Invite the cult members to consider what you have said, and tell them you will pray for them.

Often the teaching of a cult is like a fire that consumes everything in its path. We can stop that fire only by using the fire of the Holy Spirit, speaking through God's Word of truth about Jesus Christ. Point cult members to Jesus' death on the cross for your sins, and share with them the certainty you have of your forgiveness and eternal life. And by all means leave the door open for further conversations. Pray for them.

REMEMBER

You, dear children, are from God, and have overcome them, because the one who is in you is greater than the one who is in the world.
1 John 4:4

FOR NEXT TIME

What do you know about Jehovah's Witnesses? Make notes to summarize things you can recall.

Session 21

Is Christ God or Man?
The Jehovah's Witnesses

AT YOUR DOOR

Have you ever answered the door and discovered one or two ordinary-looking people who want to talk to you about religion? Perhaps they asked you questions about your life or offered you a copy of a magazine from their briefcases. These people may be Mormons or Jehovah's Witnesses. Both spend time sharing their faith through door-to-door witnessing.

ATTACKING YOU, HEAD ON!

Some enemies attack you from behind, in secret. Others go straight for your head, the most visible and vulnerable part of your body. If they succeed in defeating our head, they have won everything!

This is also the case with Christianity. Satan, the father of lies, constantly attacks the most visible part of our faith, our Head—Jesus Christ. Almost every cult in the world today denies that Jesus Christ is truly God. The Bible, however, clearly says: **"In Christ all the fullness of the Deity lives in bodily form"** (Colossians 2:9).

Furthermore, Jesus encouraged His followers to honor Him as they honored the Father. He said: **"The Father judges no one, but has entrusted all judgment to the Son, that all may honor the Son just as they honor the Father. He who does not honor the Son does not honor the Father, who sent Him"** (John 5:22–23).

THE HISTORY OF JEHOVAH'S WITNESSES

In 1879, after several years of Bible study, Charles Taze Russell began a magazine, *Zion's Watch Tower,* and in 1886 published his first book. Russell said that Jesus Christ is not God in human flesh, but rather a created being like the rest of us.

The Watchtower Society's second president, Joseph Franklin Rutherford, changed the name of the organization to "Jehovah's Witnesses." Rutherford exercised complete control over all spiritual and temporal matters of the Jehovah's Witnesses, with power to make all decisions.

Under the aggressive leadership of the next president, Nathan H. Knorr, the little group of Bible students blossomed from 115,000 to over two million members. It also produced its own English translation of the Bible, "The New World Translation."

The rapid growth and zealous activity of this group have been attributed to the fact that it is active in spreading the message of what it believes. Its members commit 40 hours each month to door to door witnessing and tract distribution.

Jehovah's Witnesses really have no confessions or creeds. Instead, articles in their various publications serve the same purpose. Jehovah's Witnesses consider the views presented in *The Watchtower* and *Awake* to be doctrinally correct, and believe that these words contain the same authority as if handed down from Jehovah God Himself!

JEHOVAH'S WITNESSES USE THE BIBLE

While Jehovah's Witnesses claim that the Bible is their final source of authority, their misuse of the Bible leads to their peculiar beliefs. They consistently quote the Bible without regard to the context and omit passages that clearly contradict their beliefs.

Jehovah's Witnesses deny the Trinity, since the word "Trinity" isn't in the Bible, and they believe teachings about the Trinity to be another of Satan's attempts to keep God-fearing people from knowing the truth about God. They also deny the deity of the Holy Spirit, making Him even lesser than Jesus.

Jehovah's Witnesses believe that Jesus Christ is really an incarnation of the angel Michael, who fought with Satan **(Revelation 12:7).**

They also deny the existence of hell as a place of everlasting punishment. They believe that this teaching is unscriptural, unreasonable, and contrary to the love and justice of God. This is consistent with their understanding of sin. Jehovah's Witnesses do not believe that sin is an offense against the holy and righteous will of God. They believe that each person, by his or her own obedience, can become worthy to enter eternal life.

Jehovah's Witnesses also deny the resurrection of Christ from the dead. They will admit that Christ came out of the grave, but only as a spirit. Notice how they contradict **Luke 24:36–39; John 20:25–29; and Revelation 1:17–18.**

Jehovah's Witnesses insist on interpreting Bible prophecies literally. Such an interpretation of **Revelation 14:1** leads them to believe that the actual number of the "saved" will be 144,000.

Ever since Christ left, promising His return **(John 14:3; Acts 1:11),** people have wondered *when* He will return. Jehovah's Witnesses predicted His visible return in 1914, but when that failed, they said He returned invisibly! They again predicted a visible vindication of their prophecies when Christ would show Himself in 1925, but that too failed. The failure of another prediction of His return set for 1975 has dampened the spirits of some Witnesses, and some feel that their numbers may be dwindling as a result of their failure to interpret the Bible correctly.

CHRISTIANS ALSO USE THEIR BIBLES!

It is important to remember, when confronted by Jehovah's Witnesses, not to panic. Because they know selected Bible verses so well, many well-intentioned Christians become overwhelmed by them and listen to what they have to say. Simply by the sheer weight of conviction and convincing, many Christians have been led astray.

Be sure to check in context *every* Bible verse they quote to you. They are usually willing to spend the time with you, so sit down with your Bible and theirs. Compare the verses they speak about. Read the verses before and after the verse they center on. Often such a context study will bring their false interpretation to light.

Consider **John 14:28,** for example (one of their favorite verses). While Jesus clearly says, **"The Father is greater than I,"** a careful reading of the entire chapter reveals that He willingly took on a subordinate role so He could become our Savior. Note that Jesus also stresses the inaccessibility of the Father without Him **(verse 6)** and the fact that They exist within each other **(verse 11).** If we are to accept the witnesses' interpretation of **John 14:28** "out of context," ask them also to accept the exact wording of **John 10:30** and **17:22!**

Jehovah's Witnesses also like to look at the word *firstborn* in **Colossians 1:15.** This they feel makes Christ *created,* and therefore inferior to God. Notice that in the same context **(verses 16–17)** Paul also says that Christ actually is the Creator of all things! The word *firstborn* means *choicest.* Christ is the best—quite the opposite from what they try to imply from the verse!

The *New World Translation* of **John 1:1** ("The word was a god") has caused all sorts of difficulties. Totally unsupported by the rest of the Bible, this translation places Jesus in a position lower than Jehovah God! This translation, which does not agree with the original language, denies the main truth of this verse, namely, that "Jesus Christ is true God!" **"The Word was God"** (John 1:1).

JESUS CHRIST IS OUR HEAD THE FIRST, THE LAST THE LIVING ONE

1. Write a short essay about our Head, Jesus Christ. Before you begin, read **Ephesians 1:22; 2:4–7, 20; 4:15;** and **Colossians 1:18.**

2. Write a short essay about Jesus Christ, the first, the last, the living One. Before you begin, read **Revelation 1:8, 17–18; 22:12–13;** and **Hebrews 9:11–12, 23–28.**

WHAT DO YOU SAY TO SOMEONE WHO KNOCKS?

Peter reminds us: **"Always be prepared to give an answer to everyone who asks you to give the reason for the hope that you have. But do this with gentleness and respect"** (1 Peter 3:15). Don't share with Jehovah's Witnesses just to disprove them or trip them up! Show Jesus to them. Help them see His outstretched arms and feel His embrace. Desire that they not only lay aside all their efforts but also sink into His comforting arms of love and forgiveness, awaiting the blessed reunion that all believers will share with Him one day. Let them see that your hope is in Jesus!

REMEMBER

God so loved the world that He gave His one and only Son, that whoever believes in Him shall not perish but have eternal life.

John 3:16

FOR NEXT TIME

Jehovah's Witnesses deny the Trinity. Can you name other religions that emphasize a denial of the Trinity of God?

Session 22

Anti-Trinitarianism: Who Is God?

WHO IS GOD?

Hear, O Israel: The Lord our God, the Lord is one.
Deuteronomy 6:4

The Athanasian Creed, developed between the third and ninth centuries, gives a clear description of how the early church understood God. It begins this way:

"Whoever will be saved shall, above all else, hold the catholic faith.

"Which faith, except everyone keeps whole and undefiled, without doubt he will perish eternally.

"And the catholic faith is this, that we worship one God in three persons and three persons in one God, neither confusing the persons nor dividing the substance."

The Bible doesn't describe God in exactly these words. Instead, the Bible simply records God's own self-revelation. God describes Himself as Father, Son, and Holy Spirit. Each is wholly God; yet without any one part, the Godhead would be incomplete. Each *Person* of this Trinity has a special function, and each of these functions is extremely important to us.

In your notebook write a paragraph that describes why you think it is important to maintain faith in God as three Persons.

One of the best-known Bible passages that describes the Trinity is **Matthew 28:19–20.** Jesus told His disciples, **"Go and make disciples of all nations, baptizing them in the name of the Father and of the Son and of the Holy Spirit, and teaching them to obey everything I have commanded you."** Remember, this is the way God has revealed Himself to us!

THE FATHER IS GOD

Look at the entire Athanasian Creed. (It appears in *Lutheran Worship*, pp. 134–135, and *The Lutheran Hymnal,* page 53.) Which words describe the Father? What do those words mean?

Read **1 Peter 1:17.** The fact that Peter encouraged his readers to call on the Father at any time suggests that he and they had some kind of faith in God's ability to hear their requests. Does God hear every prayer? Does He answer every prayer? How do you know He hears and answers your prayers?

According to **Galatians 1:1,** the apostle Paul acknowledges that he was sent by God the Father. How might this help his believability among people living in the province of Galatia?

Which term from the Athanasian Creed, descriptive of God the Father, assures us that He hears and answers all prayers? Why is this important to you? What would happen to your prayer life if you weren't certain?

THE SON IS GOD

Perhaps Paul is reacting to an organized group that denied the deity of Christ when, in **Colossians 2:9,** he said: **"In Christ all the fullness of the Deity lives in bodily form."** If Christ is truly God, all the characteristics of the Father should also be present in Jesus. Look at the miracles of Jesus (for example, **John 2:1–11; 4:43–54**). Christ is both almighty and all-knowing!

In **Philippians 2:5–11** Paul points out that, while Christ had all the power and glory of the Godhead, He humbled Himself and became a human being, like us. He is both a real human person and at the same time God!

THE HOLY SPIRIT IS GOD

Some people have a great deal of difficulty thinking of the Third Person of the Trinity as a Person. In fact, many people refer to the Spirit as a thing—an *it.* Yet Scripture clearly uses the same words to describe this Third Person of the Trinity as it uses to describe the First Person and the Second Person. (See, for example, **John 14:17.**)

The Spirit has divine names **(1 Corinthians 3:16)** and, like the other Persons, knows all things **(2:9–10).** And not only does He know all things, but He will remind us of everything Jesus has taught us **(John 14:16–26).**

In Acts 5:1–11 we learn that Ananias and his wife, Sapphira, had agreed to sell some property and supposedly give it all to the Lord. But when they sold the property, they held some back for themselves, and Ananias presented the remaining money to God's apostles. When asked if this was all the money, he lied and said it was. Peter accused Ananias of lying to the Holy Spirit. In the next verse **(5:4)** Peter reminded Ananias that he hadn't lied simply to people, but to God. So the Holy Spirit *is* also God!

THE UNITARIAN CHURCH

It is quite obvious from the name that, among other things, the Unitarian church denies the Trinity. Although the first Unitarian society was organized in the United States in 1825, the anti-Trinitarian movement had already existed here for a long time. Early U. S. Unitarians felt that the Trinity was an offense to any intelligent person, and that such a teaching would allow polytheism.

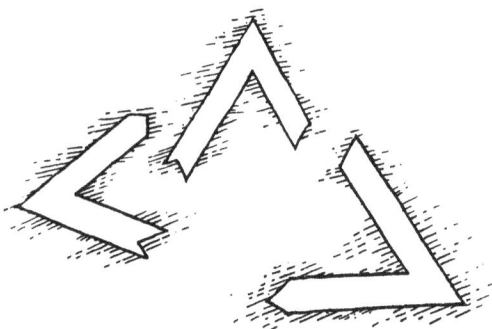

One second- and third-century heresy (*Monarchianism*) was a belief in a unified deity. Believing that God was a unified king, followers of this teaching reacted against polytheism, and said that God was one (monotheism). In the 16th century, a man named F. P. Sozzini denied the deity of Christ and later the Trinity. There were many Unitarian Christian churches in Poland in the 17th century. A teaching known as *Socinianism*—named after Sozzini (Socinus in Latin)—ultimately ignored Christ's life and death altogether and came to include a belief that people could, by being good, save themselves.

It was a short step from Socinianism to the sermon of William Ellery Channing, in 1819 at Harvard College, in which he called for a simplification of the Trinity to a Unity. Actually, many modern Unitarians accept the name *Unitarian* only under protest. They feel that even this name sounds too much like Trinitarianism.

In 1961 the Unitarians merged with another group, the *Universalists*. Universalists find the Biblical concept of hell and eternal punishment inconsistent with their view of God. They believe that ultimately everyone will be saved and go to heaven.

Other teachings that characterize the Unitarian societies are the lack of a universal creed, belief in the Fatherhood of God, and belief that each individual can believe as he or she wishes, that everyone may be divine in the same sense that Jesus was divine, that the purpose of all religion is to help improve and perfect people, and that a person can get right with God by his or her own character.

TEST THE SPIRITS

Once again it is necessary to heed the words of John: **"Test the spirits to see whether they are from God . . . . Every spirit that acknowledges that Jesus Christ has come in the flesh is from God, but every spirit that does not acknowledge Jesus is not from God"** (1 John 4:1–3).

Do you think a group that denies the Holy Trinity or that believes in salvation simply by improving people's character, can be called Christian? Compare its teachings with the claims that Jesus made. Then thank God for providing you with the truth about Jesus, who died and rose so that, when you die, you too can rise and live with Him forever.

REMEMBER

The next day John saw Jesus coming toward him and said, "Look, the Lamb of God, who takes away the sin of the world!"

John 1:29

FOR NEXT TIME

See if you can list any religious groups that have sacred writings they believe are on the same level or higher than Holy Scripture.

Session 23

Mormonism: New Revelation Is Better Than the Old?

MORMON HISTORY

The Church of Jesus Christ of Latter-day Saints (commonly known as Mormons) holds that God has given them special revelations beyond the Bible. In fact, they believe that *The Book of Mormon* actually completes the Bible, just as the ordinances and rituals of their church complete the sacrifice of Christ's death on the cross.

The Book of Mormon contains an early history of two groups of people who left Palestine and traveled to the western hemisphere, ultimately settling in North America. One group left the tower of Babel in 2250 B.C. and traveled first to Europe, later to Central America. Its leader, a prophet named Mormon, recorded the history of these people, called "the Jaredites," in *The Book of Mormon.* They were later destroyed because of their unfaithfulness.

A second group, led by Nephi, left Jerusalem in about 600 B.C. Crossing the Pacific Ocean, it settled in what is now Peru. This group divided into two warring camps, the Nephites and the Lamanites. The Lamanites were cursed for their evil deeds, and this curse resulted in their dark skins. According to Mormon beliefs, the Lamanites were Indians. When they traveled to North America, Jesus Christ personally visited both groups. The Nephites were destroyed by the Lamanites in a great battle near the hill Cumorah, at Palmyra, NY, in A. D. 385.

In 1827 a young treasure hunter, Joseph Smith Jr., said that he discovered the record of the early Mormons. According to Smith this record—recorded on thin metal plates, gold in appearance, and written in "reformed Egyptian"—was discovered buried in the same hill. Smith claimed he was visited by an angel, Moroni, who gave him directions both for finding and translating these strange tablets. The chest containing Mormon's writings also contained a special pair of gold spectacles. When worn, these glasses allowed anyone to translate and understand the writings.

Smith had been wondering which of the many churches he should join. The angel told him that it was God's will for him to form a new church, especially fit for these *latter days.* This *restoration* church would be a uniquely American church and would allow Smith and his followers to understand the truth about God.

Smith convinced several of his friends of the authenticity of this book. The plates, he said, were returned to Moroni after the translation was finished. One of Smith's friends sold his farm and financed Smith's translation of *The Book of Mormon,* which was published for the first time in 1830.

After a series of moves, and after Smith was lynched at Carthage, IL, in 1844, one group of his followers (The Church of Jesus Christ of Latter-day Saints), led by Brigham Young, settled in Utah. Another (smaller) group (the Reorganized Church of Jesus Christ of the Latter Day Saints) followed Smith's son and settled in Independence, MO. Each felt that the location of its headquarters was the exact spot to which Jesus Christ would return visibly.

WHAT DO MORMONS BELIEVE?

Many people are shocked when they hear the Mormons labeled a cult. They seem so nice! Indeed, they tend to be nice, moral people, but their doctrines and teachings depart quite far from historical Christian teachings. Therefore the Mormons can properly be considered a cult.

Mormons believe, for example, that God has a flesh-and-blood body, evolved from mortal human beings, and is actually not one, but many gods. Every male Mormon actually dedicates his life to becoming a part of this polytheistic godhead. This is called "Eternal Progression."

Similarly, Mormons believe that Jesus was simply a man, who evolved to become a god. He is only one god among many, and actually a brother of Satan. Mormons claim that Jesus was a polygamist, who was born of a physical union of Joseph and Mary. The blood of Jesus Christ is considered important, but only in cleansing *some* sin.

Mormons believe that salvation can be obtained only by keeping the laws and ordinances of the church.

Their *Articles of Faith* state: "We believe that through the atonement of Christ, all mankind will be saved, by obedience to the laws and ordinances of the gospel."One Mormon tract says, "Much of what the churches teach about faith in Christ is so obviously false that to believe it is to lose salvation. For instance, some say that simply to believe in Jesus is to be saved" (*Lutheran Witness,* October 1986, pp. 18–19. Used by permission of Concordia Publishing House.)

Contrast this with Christ's statement in **Mark 16:16** or the words of the apostle Paul in **Ephesians 2:8–10!** Rather than offering comfort, a salvation that is not free produces only anxiety and worry. Jesus teaches us that our works aren't something to boast about, but rather fruits of faith, that flow from our belief and trust in Him **(Matthew 7:17–20)**.

Mormons practice *sealed marriages,* which they believe last for eternity, and *baptism for the dead,* in which non-Mormon ancestors can be baptized into heaven by substituting their live descendants in the ritual. Loosely based on **1 Corinthians 15:29,** this baptism involves complicated genealogical charts. The assembling of these charts and baptizing of the dead has become a major part of the work of the Mormon church.

Closely related to this is the Mormon view of a three-level heaven. Only true Mormons can ever enter into the highest level, called *celestial.* Other Christians, called "Gentiles" by the Mormons, will enter into a *terrestrial* heaven, which is somewhat lower. All those currently in hell will be relegated to a *telestial* heaven, awaiting a final resurrection of all flesh.

Mormons shun the use of alcohol, tobacco, and all caffeine products. Every Mormon young person is required to commit (and finance) two years of life to a missionary effort somewhere in the world.

"A NEW, BETTER REVELATION"

One of the most distinctive features of the Mormon church is its belief that *The Book of Mormon* is a second, complete revelation of God's truth. Orson Pratt, a leader in the Mormon church, said of the Bible, "Who, in his right mind, could for one moment suppose the Bible in its present form to be a perfect guide? Who knows that even one verse of the whole Bible has escaped pollution?" (*Lutheran Witness,* October 1986, page 5)

Mormons look to human reason, believing that *The Book of Mormon* (obviously written by Joseph Smith!) is better than, and actually completes, the Bible.

Look at what God's Word says about itself. Jesus says that the Word of His Father is truth **(John 17:17).**

Peter claims that it lasts forever **(1 Peter 1:25).** Paul reminds us that all of the sacred writings, called simply *Scriptures,* are inspired by God and useful for teaching, correction, and a general building up of the person who is devoted to God **(2 Timothy 3:16).** Scripture didn't just occur because some people got the idea to write it, but because the Holy Spirit inspired them to write down God's own words **(2 Peter 1:21).**

Rather than looking for other revelations of His will, Jesus urged His disciples to continue studying His Word **(John 8:31).** In fact, the Word of God is like a light, to show us the way to go, lighting up the obstacles so we can avoid them **(Psalm 119:105).** Paul issued a warning against some, like the Mormons, who might come with another gospel **(Galatians 1:8–9).** By suggesting that people must keep the laws in order to be saved, the Mormons are advocating just such a gospel and place themselves under the warning issued in **Revelation 22:18–19.**

Perhaps we all need to hear the words of the Father once again. At the baptism of His Son and again at His transfiguration, our God said: **"This is My Son, whom I love; with Him I am well pleased. Listen to Him!"** (Matthew 3:17; 17:5). Only through His shed blood can we receive eternal life! As we follow Him, we will make a powerful witness to our Mormon friends. We may encourage them to join us in listening to Jesus. Pray that they, too, will hear Jesus and, believing in Him, live forever.

REMEMBER

The Father . . . has entrusted all judgment to the Son, that all may honor the Son just as they honor the Father. He who does not honor the Son does not honor the Father, who sent Him.
John 5:22–23

You diligently study the Scriptures because you think that by them you possess eternal life. These are the Scriptures that testify about Me, yet you refuse to come to Me to have life.
John 5:39–40

FOR NEXT TIME

Have you ever heard anything on radio or TV about the Worldwide Church of God or a preacher named Armstrong? Check your local radio and TV listings to see if such a program is being aired in your area. Check your library to see if there are any materials available about this cult. Also, see what you can find about the so-called *ten lost tribes of Israel.*

Session 24

Worldwide Church of God: A Distortion of the Truth

ALL ISRAEL WILL BE SAVED

I do not want you to be ignorant of this mystery, brothers, so that you may not be conceited: Israel has experienced a hardening in part until the full number of the Gentiles has come in. And so all Israel will be saved, as it is written: "The deliverer will come from Zion; He will turn godlessness away from Jacob. And this is My covenant with them when I take away their sins."

Romans 11:25–27

THAT WHICH WAS LOST HAS BEEN FOUND!

Have you ever prepared to play a card game, counted the cards, and found that the deck wasn't complete? Did you ever get all ready to play a game such as checkers, only to discover that you didn't have all the pieces? Nearly everyone has worked on a complicated jigsaw puzzle, only to discover that one or two pieces are missing. How frustrating!

At least one rapidly growing American religious group relies on this concept of "lostness" to attract people into their midst. The Worldwide Church of God believes that the people of England and America are actually the ten lost tribes of Israel. This church teaches that the Gospel wasn't preached anywhere on earth from the destruction of Jerusalem by the Romans until 1934, when Herbert W. Armstrong founded his church.(The Worldwide Church of God also appeals to many because—in contrast to most religious groups—it asks for no money from potential converts. Of course, the church demands *extensive* offerings later, especially by insisting on strict obedience to Old Testament laws.)

According to Armstrong, the Old Testament Hebrew people were carried off into captivity in two successive sweeps of Palestine. In 721 B. C. the ten tribes in the Northern Kingdom were exiled by the invading Assyrian armies from the north. Slightly more than a hundred years later the two remaining tribes were taken into exile by the Babylonians.

Armstrong taught that the present-day Jews come from the two tribes removed to Babylon. Most of the other ten tribes mixed with their captives, but some wandered across Europe. They became the ancestors of the Saxons in Germany. When these Saxons captured England, they became known as the Anglo-Saxons. Since the United States was first colonized by the English, the Americans and the British make up two of those ten lost tribes. Armstrong taught that the United States is actually the lost tribe of Manasseh, and Great Britain is actually Ephraim.

HISTORY OF THE WORLDWIDE CHURCH OF GOD

Herbert W. Armstrong, at one time a pastor of the Church of God (Adventist), founded his own church in 1934. He spread his message through radio programs entitled *The World Tomorrow* and through a slick magazine entitled *The Plain Truth.* In 1947 Armstrong opened the church's Ambassador College in Pasadena, CA. Later, television enhanced his ministry.

A son, Garner Ted Armstrong, worked with his father at times, though the relationship was often stormy. Finally, in 1978, he founded his own church, The Church of God International.

A group like the Worldwide Church of God thrives partly because it claims to have roots that go back to ancient Israel. And it claims to be the only original church. With exclusive claims similar to those of the Jehovah's Witnesses and the Mormons, Armstrong has built a little empire of local congregations.

Armstrong taught that God allowed two cycles of 19 years of ministry. These stretched from Christ's ascension in A. D. 31 until Jerusalem was attacked and destroyed by the Romans in 69 (Armstrong's date). The voice of God was then silent on the earth until 1934. This time God spoke to Herbert W. Armstrong. Then, Armstrong taught, God allowed two more 19-year cycles of ministry for the church on earth. These were to be completed in 1972, and Christ was to return to earth a second time to judge. During these two 19-year pe-

Since Armstrong's prophecy failed, he twice more predicted the return of Christ to earth. With each failure he provided more arguments and explanations. The Worldwide Church of God continues aggressive activity, though the founder and driving force died in 1986.

The Worldwide Church of God offers its magazines and Bible/Current Events Studies free of charge. Followers of Armstrong's kingdom are required to maintain a strict adherence to Old Testament ceremonial laws. They continue to carry out his dictates methodically, oblivious to the fact that the very Bible they study warns God's people of groups such as theirs. Apparently the people feel sure of their salvation, since Armstrong clearly spelled out the rules they must follow and they fanatically try to follow those rules. Furthermore, many appreciated Armstrong because he quoted Scripture extensively (often in total disregard of its context or meaning).

THE BIBLE AND ARMSTRONG

Like other cults, Armstrong attacked many orthodox Christian doctrines. He taught that God is a *family* or plurality of gods, *not* necessarily a Trinity. (See session 22 to review the falseness of such a teaching.)

Armstrong taught salvation by works. "Salvation, then, is a process! But how the God of this world would blind your eyes to that! He tries to deceive you into thinking all there is to it is just 'accepting Christ' with 'no works'—and presto-chango, you are pronounced 'saved.' But the Bible reveals that none is yet 'saved' " (Herbert W. Armstrong, *Why Were You Born?*, p. 11, as quoted in *Handbook of Religions,* McDowell, p. 11). But, consider **Ephesians 2:8–10** and **Titus 3:5.** People are saved by the grace and mercy of Christ, and not by their own efforts.

Armstrong interpreted **Matthew 5:5** and **Revelation 5:10** to mean that the eternal kingdom of God is here on earth, and not in heaven. He often quoted **Luke 23:43** and **2 Corinthians 5:8** to substantiate this. Armstrong also quoted **2 Timothy 4:8** to prove that God's kingdom won't be established until "that day"—not before.

Contrast that to Christ's promise that His kingdom would be in His disciples' midst, that it was spiritual, and not of this world **(Matthew 18:20; John 18:36).** Even Jesus' disciples, after spending three years with them, misinterpreted Him and were looking for a physical kingdom. Note Christ's direction to them **(Acts 1:6–8).** Christ's kingdom will spread and grow mysteriously, like the yeast in a piece of dough **(Matthew 13:33).**

Like many other cultic leaders, Armstrong denied the existence of hell as being inconsistent with God's love and grace. Recall, however, that people go to hell because they reject Christ **(Mark 16:16).**

Armstrong made many specific promises and predicted the future. We have already mentioned his prediction of Christ's return in 1972. In 1967 Armstrong repeated his promise, predicted droughts, famine, and disease epidemics within four years. When his predictions failed to materialize, he explained that he was not a prophet of God, but only a messenger.

Compare Armstrong with God's true test of a prophet of God **(Deuteronomy 18:21–22).** A true prophet *always* correctly predicts, and his predictions *always* come true. Not so with Armstrong!

When you have an opportunity to witness to Armstrong's followers, direct them to God's grace, as demonstrated by Christ's blood shed on Calvary's cross. No amount of arguing can ever convince anyone. Only the Holy Spirit can work faith, operating through God's Word **(1 Corinthians 12:3).** Share the word about the living Word, Jesus!

REMEMBER

You are all sons of God through faith in Christ Jesus, for all of you who were baptized into Christ have clothed yourselves with Christ. There is neither Jew nor Greek, slave nor free, male nor female, for you are all one in Christ Jesus.
Galatians 3:26–28

FOR NEXT TIME

The church season of Advent, just before Christmas, means that Christ is *coming*. What do Adventist churches stand for? Can you name any Adventist churches?

Session 25

Adventists: Jesus Is Coming Again, but When?

DATE-SETTING

The Seventh-day Adventists are distinctive because of the importance of date-setting in their early history. They had their beginnings in the teachings of a Baptist preacher, William Miller, in the early part of the 19th century. Because of his dynamic preaching and his convincing arguments for the early return of Christ, Miller drew large numbers of Christians from other churches.

In 1818 Miller interpreted **Daniel 8:13–14** to mean that Christ's final coming would occur sometime between March 21, 1843, and March 21, 1844. When these dates had passed, he set another date, Oct. 22, 1844. When this date also passed, many of Miller's disappointed followers returned to the churches they had left. But many of them continued to set dates for Christ's return.

Is there anything wrong with setting a date for Jesus' return? Can you remember Jesus' own caution about it? Read **Matthew 24:36, 42; Mark 13:32–33**. God obviously doesn't feel that it is necessary for us to know when Christ will return. We need only know *that* He is coming back, and to be ready **(Matthew 25:13)**.

Though Adventists claim that theirs is a noncredal church, they have many doctrines that distinguish it from other groups. The date-setting and divisions of the early Adventists did create one of the largest churches that began in the United States. But there are other interesting features of the Adventist Church.

ANOTHER GOSPEL?

"Formerly, when you did not know God, you were slaves to those who by nature are not gods. But now that you know God—or rather are known by God—how is it that you are turning back to those weak and miserable principles? Do you wish to be enslaved by them all over again? You are observing special days and months and seasons and years! I fear for you, that somehow I have wasted my efforts on you" (Galatians 4:8–10).

What makes someone a Christian? Suppose you asked that question of someone. Imagine the person said, "A Christian is a person who believes that Jesus Christ is his or her Savior from sin." What would you think of such a response? is it correct? What Bible verses can you remember that support this answer? Suppose the cross in the picture on this page represents that answer.

The next person says, "A Christian is a person who believes in Jesus Christ as Savior from sin and keeps the Ten Commandments." Is this answer right? Imagine that the little plus signs to the right of the cross in the picture represent the keeping of the Ten Commandments.

A third person might answer the question by saying, "Christians are people who believe in Jesus as their Savior from sin and who don't drink or smoke." Could this person also be a Christian? Imagine that the little minus signs to the left of the cross represent avoiding drinking and smoking.

Do you notice what happens to your eyes when you look at those tiny little signs on each side of the cross? Your attention shifts, doesn't it? You have to take your eyes off the cross in order to talk about the things a Christian should or shouldn't do. What do you think the pluses and minuses mean? Why do you suppose there are question marks by all the pluses and minuses?

When people make additional requirements for being a Christian, they create doubt in the mind of a believer. The attention is shifted off the cross (representing something Jesus has already done for us) and onto something we have yet to do. Doubts and questions are raised. Is all drinking wrong? What if we have sinned in the past? Are you comfortable in saying you are absolutely certain you will go to heaven when you die?

Some people feel that Seventh-day Adventists emphasize good works and confuse believers about the certainty of heaven. As indicated above, that certainly happens. Their official teachings, however, state that they believe they are saved by grace, as the Bible teaches.

THE SEVENTH DAY

One teaching of the Seventh-day Adventists that often confuses people is their insistence on worshiping on the Seventh Day, or Saturday.

Do you remember the Third Commandment? In **Exodus 20:8** God said, "Remember the Sabbath Day by keeping it holy." According to this commandment, on what day do you think God wants us to worship Him? Do you think God prefers Saturday over Sunday?

Do you remember the explanation of the Third Commandment from Luther's Small Catechism? "We should fear and love God that we may not despise preaching and His Word, but hold sacred and gladly hear and learn it." What do you think is God's goal for our celebration of the Sabbath day? Of course God wants us to worship Him! But do you think that the day

of the week is really important? Shouldn't we worship Him all the time?

In **Mark 2:23–28** we read of the accusations brought against Jesus because He and His disciples did not follow the old rules for the Sabbath. Those rules, however, foreshadowed the One who now had come, and **"the Son of Man is Lord even of the Sabbath" (verse 28).** Galatians 4:8–10 also shows that God no longer requires us to choose Saturday as our day of worship. We find another clear statement of that message in **Colossians 2:16–17.**

ARE ADVENTISTS CHRISTIAN?

Officially, the Adventist Church is a Christian church. But when Adventists discuss Bible teachings—especially the subject of salvation—with other Christians, issues may be clouded. They teach that salvation is a gift of God, available to people only through faith in Jesus Christ. It often seems, though, that they require more than faith in Jesus for salvation, so one might call the Adventist Church a sect or even a cult. Obviously, some members of some Adventist churches have produced *another gospel* by attaching additional requirements for salvation.

As you meet and talk to Adventists, you need to find out what they are trusting in for salvation. If they are trusting completely in Jesus as Savior from sin, rejoice in the faith God has given them. If they are uncertain, because of additional requirements that have been added to faith in Jesus, share your certainty with them. Point them to the Savior.

REMEMBER

If you confess with your mouth, "Jesus is Lord," and believe in your heart that God raised Him from the dead, you will be saved.
Romans 10:9

FOR NEXT TIME

What is humanism? Write a definition of humanism in your notebook. What about humanism makes it particularly dangerous?

Session 26

Humanism: A House Built on Sand!

WISDOM OF THE FOOLISH?

The message of the cross is foolishness to those who are perishing, but to us who are being saved, it is the power of God. For it is written: "I will destroy the wisdom of the wise; the intelligence of the intelligent I will frustrate." Where is the wise man? Where is the scholar? Where is the philosopher of this age? Has not God made foolish the wisdom of the world? For since in the wisdom of God the world through its wisdom did not know Him, God was pleased through the foolishness of what was preached to save those who believe. Jews demand miraculous signs and Greeks look for wisdom, but we preach Christ crucified: a stumbling block to Jews and foolishness to Gentiles, but those whom God has called, both Jews and Greeks, Christ the power of God and the wisdom of God. For the foolishness of God is wiser than man's wisdom, and the weakness of God is stronger than man's strength.

1 Corinthians 1:18–25

HOW WISE AND POWERFUL IS THE CHRIST?

Perhaps you've read a newspaper or magazine article about one country arming itself against another. Perhaps you've thought about the military capabilities that the various countries on earth now possess. Then consider the power of the love of Jesus Christ. Which is greater? Consider the following, called simply "One Solitary Life."

He was born in an obscure village, the child of a peasant woman. He grew up in another village, where He worked in a carpenter shop until He was thirty. Then for three years He was an itinerant preacher. He never wrote a book. He never held an office. He never had a family or owned a home. He didn't go to college. He never visited a big city. He never traveled two hundred miles from the place where He was born. He did none of the things that usually accompany greatness. He had no credentials but Himself. He was only thirty-three years old when the tide of public opinion turned against Him. His friends ran away. One of them denied Him.

He was turned over to His enemies and went through the mockery of a trial. He was nailed to a cross between two thieves. While He was dying His executioners gambled for His garments, the only property He had on earth. When He was dead, He was laid in a borrowed grave through the pity of a friend. Nineteen centuries have come and gone, and today He is the central figure of the human race. All the armies that ever marched, all the navies that ever sailed, all the parliaments that ever sat, all the kings that ever reigned, put together, have not affected the life of man on this earth as much as that one solitary life!

What is more important: wisdom as the world sees it, or God's wisdom? power as the world considers it, or as God knows it exists? Consider, for example, the authority of the Roman governor Pilate, who said to Jesus, **"Don't You realize I have power either to free You or to crucify You?" (John 19:10).** Is power something people only think they have, or is it an ability that only God can give? Think about it! Is wisdom the intellectual ability, as the Scarecrow in *The Wizard of Oz* said, to "think thoughts I've never thought before"? Or can only God give the wisdom and intelligence that apprehends God and the solutions He wants us to discover? What do you think?

THE HUMANIST CREED IN BRIEF

Following is a summary of the 17 points of *Humanist Manifesto II (1973)*. They are divided into six general groups. At the end of each section we have listed Scriptures related to the issue. These Scriptures, of course, do not appear in the *Manifesto*.

Consider each proposition as a true/false statement. Then study the Scriptures. Can you add other passages that show the errors of the humanist philosophy?

Religion

1. Traditional, dogmatic religions place God above human needs and do a disservice to the human species.

2. Promises of immortal salvation or fear of eternal damnation are both illusory and harmful.

Genesis 1:1; John 1:1–3; Acts 17:24–28; Isaiah 53:6; John 3:16; Ephesians 2:8–10.

Philosophy

3. Moral values derive their source from human experience. All ethics are situational.

4. Reason and intelligence are the most effective instruments available.

Hebrews 13:8; Isaiah 55:8; Proverbs 14:12; Ephesians 4:17–18.

Humanity

5. The central and most important value is the dignity of the individual person.

6. Intolerant attitudes, often encouraged by orthodox religions, unduly repress sexual conduct.

1 Corinthians 8:4; Exodus 20:1–6, 14; Matthew 5:27–30; Proverbs 5:18–19.

Society

7. True personal freedom results only when the individual has experienced a full range of civil liberties in all societies.

8. People everywhere must be committed to an open and democratic society.

9. The separation of church and state is imperative for maximum freedom to occur in a society.

10. A society should be evaluated not in theory, but in the sense of economic well-being achieved for all its members.

11. Moral equality can only be furthered when all discrimination is eliminated.

James 3:5–12; 1 Corinthians 8:9–13; Matthew 20:20–28; 22:15–22; Romans 13:1–7; Luke 3:11–17; Matthew 25:40; 9:13; 12:7; Galatians 3:28.

One-World Government

12. We deplore the division of humankind on nationalistic grounds.

13. The world community must renounce violence and force as a method of solving international disputes.

14. The world must engage in cooperative planning concerning the use of rapidly depleting resources.

15. The problems of economic development can no longer be handled or resolved by one nation alone.

Galatians 3:28; 6:10; Matthew 5:38–47; Luke 14:28–33; 1 Corinthians 1:19–20, 25; 4:1; 10:31; 12:12–13, 27–31; Matthew 24:45–51; 25:14–30, 40; Genesis 11:4, 8.

Science

16. Science and technology are the vital keys to human progress and development.

17. Travel and communication must be expanded beyond all frontiers.

2 Corinthians 5:16–17; Hebrews 1:1–2; 11:1–3; Philippians 1:6; Matthew 28:19–20; Romans 1:22; 1 Corinthians 1:18–25; 1 Timothy 6:20–21.

DIRECTIONS: HUMANISM AND CHRISTIANITY

After reading these 17 propositions, where do you think humanism is headed? Why is that philosophy like a house built on sand?

Do you think humanism wants to improve the quality of life for all people? If so, how does humanist thinking propose to do it? If not, can you suggest alternative ways in which the quality of life can be improved?

What about Christianity? In what direction is Christianity headed? Why do you think the followers of Jesus formed the structures of the holy Christian church? Do you think that people who make up Christian churches today want to improve the quality of life for all people? If not, what alternatives can you suggest?

We are moving swiftly and certainly toward the return of Christ to judge the world. Any group worth the name Christian senses the urgency with which this final reckoning is approaching. Any church built on the Rock, Jesus, is solidly waiting the time when He will come to claim them and others who have come to the same Rock for stability, direction, and comfort, now and forever.

REMEMBER

In the last day scoffers will come. . . . They will say, "Where is this 'coming' He promised? Every since our fathers died, everything goes on as it has since the beginning of creation." But they deliberately forget that long ago by God's word the heavens existed and the earth was formed out of water and by water. . . . In keeping with His promise we are looking forward to a new heaven and a new earth, the home of righteousness. So then, dear friends, since you are looking forward to this, make every effort to be found spotless, blameless and at peace with Him.

2 Peter 3:3–5, 13–14

Session 27

Review of Sessions 19–26

Give brief, yet complete, answers to the following questions.

1. Define "cult."

2. How do cults differ from mainline Christian denominations?

3. Use **2 Tim. 4:3–4** to explain the rapid rise of cults in America.

4. What features of cults explain how they can grow so rapidly?

5. What features about people and our society explain how cults can grow so rapidly?

6. What does it mean to test the spirits **(1 John 4:1)?**

7. Explain several *new* things that cults offer.

8. Explain several *immediate* things that cults offer.

9. Explain several *false* things that cults offer.

10. What are some things most cults require of all new recruits?

11. List several main teachings of the Jehovah's Witnesses that conflict with Scripture.

12. Explain how Jehovah's Witnesses misinterpret **John 1:1.**

13. Explain how you would reconcile **John 10:30** and **14:28** to a Jehovah's Witness at your door.

14. List and explain three Bible passages you would use in witnessing to your faith in Jesus when speaking to a Jehovah's Witness.

15. Relate specific verses from **Hebrews 7–10** that testify to your belief that Jesus' shed blood was a sacrifice for your sins.

16. List and explain four Bible verses that describe God as triune.

17. Describe God the Father and the major work performed by Him.

18. Describe God the Son and the major work performed by Him.

19. Describe God the Holy Spirit and the major work performed by Him.

20. Explain major conflicts between the Unitarian Church and Scripture.

21. Briefly tell the history of the Mormon Church.

22. What is the Mormon view of both the Bible and *The Book of Mormon?*

23. Explain the Scriptures you would use to explain to a Mormon that faith in Jesus' shed blood is all that is necessary for salvation.

24. What part has the belief and practice of polygamy played in the development of the Mormon church?

25. Show that *The Book of Mormon* is not God's Word, nor is it a more important authority.

26. Briefly tell the history of The Worldwide Church of God and its founder.

27. What are the beliefs of the Worldwide Church of God as they refer to the tribes of ancient Israel?

28. What did Armstrong teach about God's kingdom, especially as he interpreted **Matthew 5:5** and **Revelation 5:10?**

29. What was the system of date-setting and 19-year cycles taught by Armstrong?

30. How can you use **Deuteronomy 18:21–22** to explain that Armstrong was not a prophet of the true God?

31. What do Seventh-day Adventists teach about worship on Saturday?

32. What do Seventh-day Adventists teach about the return of Christ to earth?

33. Explain how some Seventh-day Adventists may give the impression that people can be saved by doing good works.

34. What difficulties do Seventh-day Adventists get into with date-setting?

35. Define humanism.

36. Explain the danger humanism holds for Christianity.

37. For each of the six categories in *Humanist Manifesto II* state humanism's contradiction of Christianity, and explain one or more Bible verses that indicate the proper Biblical teaching.

38. Explain why humanism is attractive to so-called intellectuals.

39. How does **Proverbs 14:12** characterize humanism?

UNIT 5

Eastern and "New Christian" Cults

Cults like the Jehovah's Witnesses and the Mormons have been around for years. Our country is also sprinkled with many "new Christian" cults. Thousands of groups are being fed by people who were dissatisfied with their own mainline Christian denomination. Paul anticipated this when he warned Timothy about people who would have "itching ears" **(2 Timothy 4:3–4).**

Then, as if we didn't have enough religious groups in our country, leaders of several Eastern religions recognized the United States as prime territory in which to plant their groups. So several Eastern religions have also taken root here. These religions often mix elements of both Eastern and Western thought.

As you study these groups, try to imagine how different life would be if at confirmation *you* had joined one of them. Ask yourself, "Why would someone *want* to join one of these groups?"

One new issue is important in this unit. Many of the "new Christian" and Eastern cults have been accused of using coercive mind-control techniques in recruiting members for their groups. Many have questioned whether everyone who joins a cult does so freely. A similar issue surfaces when we consider how some parents, feeling that their children have been coerced or tricked into cult membership, seek to lead them out, often forcibly!

Share your thoughts and ideas about these cults. As you study this unit, celebrate the freedom you have in Jesus!

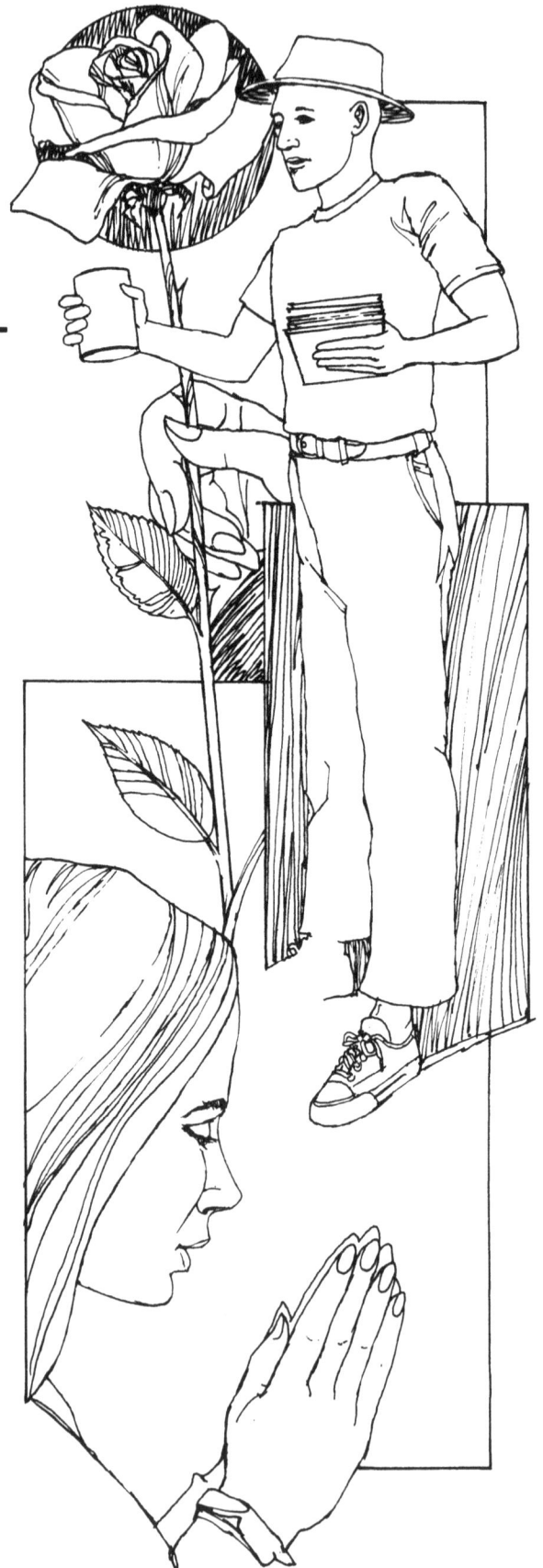

Session 28

Where Did All the New Cults Come From?

LIVING SACRIFICES

I urge you, brothers, in view of God's mercy, to offer your bodies as living sacrifices, holy and pleasing to God—this is your spiritual act of worship. Do not conform any longer to the pattern of this world, but be transformed by the renewing of your mind. Then you will be able to test and approve what God's will is—His good, pleasing and perfect will.

Romans 12:1–2

WHERE DID THEY COME FROM?

Many so called "new Christian" cults arose through the "Jesus People" movement in the late 1960s and early 1970s. This movement was more or less a spontaneous activity of young people across America who saw the organized church as ineffective.

Discouraged with the organized church, these groups encouraged public confession of faith. "Jesus freaks," as they were sometimes called, appeared on college campuses, in bus depots, on city streets, and elsewhere. Many of them eagerly distributed leaflets and shared their often newfound faith in Jesus. They were eager to "help" people less fortunate than themselves.

It appears that this "Jesus People" movement began as a reaction against the violence and sex-orientation of the "New Left." No one individual can lay official claim to originating this movement, though several cultic leaders have made that claim. As the Jesus Movement gained popularity, individuals outside the movement saw and seized an opportunity to achieve profit individually or for their pet cause by exploiting the enthusiasm of the young people within the movement.

Many "new" Eastern cults, to be discussed in Session 30, were also born during this same period. Gurus trained in Eastern religions, such as Hinduism and Buddhism, flocked to America and reaped huge profits in people and money. These groups attracted those whose religious experiences were nontraditional. The Eastern cults encouraged people to concentrate their efforts inward, toward self. They encouraged meditation and self-actualization (rather than outward service to others, a characteristic of the Jesus Movement).

WHERE ARE THEY GOING?

At first, reaction toward these groups was positive. The young people made "being a Christian" acceptable. They shared their faith and even motivated some traditional Christians to get out and share *their* faith. They showed the world that "being a Christian" could mean *peace* and *joy!*

A closer look at these newly formed groups revealed problems, however. They were too simplistic, often suggesting that "knowing Jesus" was all that mattered. They shunned organized doctrinal statements and centered their reality on their own experiences. They often talked only of the here and now, and made few plans for the future.

These groups attracted people away from traditional churches. They led recruits into the "wilderness," but then offered them nothing substantial. As frauds and pretenders infiltrated their midst, the Jesus Movement became perverted, often centering around a single person and that person's feelings and wishes. The result can be seen most clearly in groups like the Children of God, which today is known as the Family of Love.

CHILDREN OF GOD

David Berg founded the Children of God in 1968 when he and his wife moved to Huntington Beach, CA. Berg's mother was an evangelist and his father a minister. Berg himself was ordained as a pastor in the Christian and Missionary Alliance Church in 1949 but left that denomination a year later, when he had a falling out with the leadership. He believed that God had a special purpose for his life.

In 1969 a small group of people who were dissatisfied with society gathered around Berg. When Berg predicted that an earthquake would send California sliding into the ocean, he and about 50 of his followers moved to Arizona. When they disrupted worship services in churches there, they continued their wanderings. They staged demonstrations wherever they went, attracting mostly negative attention.

During this time Berg changed his name to Moses David, or "Mo," and encouraged all converts to assume a Biblical name, symbolic of their "new birth." In 1970 the little group was allowed the use of "camp" facilities belonging to TV evangelist Fred Jordan. During this time the group grew to about 250 followers, but when a disagreement with Jordan developed, they were asked to leave. From that time until the present the Children of God have wandered, forming themselves into informal "family" units of less then 12 people.

In 1978 the Children of God changed their name to the Family of Love. They boast about 7,000 members in 80 countries. "Mo," their leader, lives in seclusion in Europe, from where he directs the groups through his famous "Mo" letters.

WHAT DO GOD'S CHILDREN TEACH ABOUT HIM?

Because the Children of God have no official, dogmatic statement of faith, their theological views are somewhat vague. They believe that the letters from "Mo" are more valuable than the Bible. Although his letters are often contradictory, his followers seem to believe this is perfectly alright.

One example of a letter from "Mo" follows. See how many false or contradictory statements you can discover.

Well, if they believe in the virgin birth then they have got to believe in the divinity of Jesus, that He was partly God, even though according to some of their advocates they claim they don't. See they're contradicting their own Bible, because if He was virgin-born then He was the Son of God.

*'Even so God createth what He willeth.' In other words He, Jesus, was a creation of God. Oh, this is exactly according to Scriptures! Can you think of a verse on it? What does God's word say about Jesus? It says that He was "the beginning of the creation of God" (**Revelation 3:14**)!*

Now you know that the Catholics and some are so strong on the so-called Trinity, but I don't even believe in the Trinity. You can't find that word in the Bible, so why should I believe in it? But I believe in the Father and I believe in the Son, Jesus, and I believe in the Holy Ghost.

If you want to call it Trinity, all right, but I don't

*believe in it in some ways, the way some overemphasize and stress it, you know. You would think that Jesus just always was, just like God, but in a sense He was not until He was made man, although He was in the beginning and He was a part of God. But God's Word also says that He was in the beginning of the creation— you know where that's found? I recall it's in **Revelation** in the first two or three chapters there.*

Taken from *The Children of God: the Inside Story* by Deborah and Bill Davis. Copyright © 1984 by The Zondervan Corporation. Used by Permission.

WHAT DO THEY DO?

The Children of God are very revolutionary. As a group, they require all who join to "forsake everything" and give it to the group. They suggest that this is patterned after the New Testament Church **(Acts 2:44)**. (Note that this aspect resembles iconoclasm—session 14.) When joining the group, a person is required to renounce all former ties to family and friends. (Family and former friends would be jealous of and opposed to new relationships.)

Children of God members are very active in what they call "litnessing" (witnessing with literature—the spread of "Mo" letter tracts). They travel about, often feeding on food discarded behind restaurants and stores. They recruit people for their families, but their recruiting tactics are questionable. "Mo" encourages women cult members to engage in the practice of "flirty fishing," which involves the use of sexual seduction for recruiting.

Berg's preoccupation with sex has become more and more noticeable over a period of time. Members of this group have strayed farther and farther from the truth of the Gospel of Jesus Christ and have become more and more preoccupied with their own sinful pleasures.

REMEMBER

He is before all things, and in Him all things hold together. And He is the Head of the body, the church; He is the Beginning and the Firstborn from among the dead, so that in everything He might have the supremacy.

Colossians 1:17–18

FOR NEXT TIME

What do you know about other "new Christian" cults, such as the Unification Church, The Way International, and The People's Temple?

Session 29

In New Christian Cults, the Moon Is Not the Son!

THE VISION

On Easter Sunday, 1936, a young Presbyterian was deep in prayer on a mountainside in his native Korea. Years later the Rev. Sun Myung Moon suggested that at this point Jesus Christ first appeared to him and commissioned him to complete a task at which Jesus had failed. In preparing Moon for the great spiritual struggle that lay ahead of him, Moon suggests, Jesus directed him to establish "The Holy Spirit Association for the Unification of World Christianity."

This group teaches that Moon has succeeded where Jesus failed. According to his *Divine Principle,* Jesus succeeded in redeeming the world *spiritually,* but not physically. Moon teaches that Christ sent him marry the *perfect* wife, father the *perfect* children, and thus repopulate the world. According to Moon, true salvation can be found only in the Unification Church.

Show from Galatians 1:6–9 that this teaching contradicts the Bible.

MOON FORMS THE UNIFICATION CHURCH

In the seven years that followed his initial experience, Moon developed the contents of his *Divine Principle.* After some struggles within an extremist Pentecostal Movement, he changed his name to Sun Myung Moon (Shining Sun and Moon) and founded the Unification Church (in 1954).

In 1966 Moon's *Divine Principle* was published for the first time. In it he suggested that the sinfulness of all people was due to an illicit relationship between our first mother, Eve, and the angel Lucifer. This necessitated receiving a perfect nature by a similar sexual relationship with the perfect Messiah, Moon. A second edition of *Divine Principle,* published in 1973, plays down sexual references considerably, possibly because of the great amount of persecution Moon has received.

Moon has also developed many business interests to finance his church, and he has become very wealthy. In the 1960s Moon again launched a vigorous anticommunist campaign and supported the South Korean leader Park Chung Hee.

In 1972 Moon declared that God was directing him to the fertile mission field of the United States. He bought a 22-acre estate in Tarrytown, NY, which was to serve as the American headquarters and training center for his church. In 1975 Moon sent missionaries to 95 foreign countries. He frequently has met opposition, but it has often been countered by an incredible wave of popularity.

We may wonder how anyone with such strange teachings could attract so many people. Apparently many people in the United States are "joiners," eager to "join up" and be a part of "the group." Combine this with the fact that Moon's recruiters were trained to look for young people who were in transition situations or were undergoing identity crises. They were especially vulnerable to Moon's mind-control techniques. More about this in session 32!

MOONIE CLAIMS

The Bible and the Divine Principle

Moon frequently quotes the Bible in his teachings and in his major writing, *Divine Principle.* However, he feels his writings constitute a *new revelation* from God, that these writings circumvent the Scriptures, correct errors in them, and describe the ultimate truth that God wants His followers to know.

Contrast this with what God says in John 1:14 and 2 Timothy 3:16.

The Fall of Man

Moon teaches that although created by God, Adam and Eve were in an *unstable* condition. They were living together as brother and sister, as God's children. Lucifer, an archangel, was created as God's servant. Lucifer was jealous because Adam was God's *child* and destined to be Eve's *husband.* Lucifer seduced Eve, and the resultant race was imperfect.

Moon teaches that Christ redeemed all people from this *spiritual* fall. But Eve's subsequent physical relationship with Adam constituted a *physical* fall. It is from this *physical* fall that Moon came to redeem all people.

The Bible doesn't teach anything about a physical and a spiritual fall. What does the Bible teach in Genesis 3:1–15; Romans 5:12; and John 3:6?

The Redemption

Moon teaches that God would send a *Second Adam* to *redeem* all people, because Jesus actually failed in His task, since He was not supposed to die on the cross. Moon feels that Christ's death was a victory for Satan. Of course Moon denies the deity of Christ. Moon (according to himself) arrived on the scene to *perfect* all things, especially where Christ failed. He describes *the Lord of the Second Advent* as one who will come to perfect all imperfection. Although Moon and his followers never publicly equate Moon with this *Second Adam* or *Lord of the Second Advent*, private references to Moon make it plain they are referring to him.

How does the above contradict the Bible's clear teachings about Jesus? Consider passages such as 2 Corinthians 5:17; Hebrews 1:1–2; 2:17; 4:15; 7:26; 10:14; and Colossians 1:15–20.

Following Moon

Moon's followers are required to follow him without question. Recruitment techniques are deceptive and misleading. Those who are approached by Moonie recruiters are first evaluated according to their vulnerability and susceptibility. If they are considered to be "ripe," they are recruited. They may be invited to a free dinner. At the dinner someone speaks about the highly idealistic goals of the group, which includes the *unification* of all religions under Moon's umbrella.

Following the dinner, invitation to a weekend retreat is offered, at which time new recruits are "love-bombed" with care and attention. They are never left alone. They attend lectures and Bible studies during which the name of Moon and the Unification Church are never mentioned. In fact, it is seldom suggested that this is a church at all.

At the close of the weekend retreat, another invitation is extended. This time, the new recruits are invited to a week- or monthlong camp. Extensive indoctrination occurs at these camps. The "love-bombing" continues. Training for fund-raising takes place, and Moonie recruits are sent out in teams. Accompanied by an experienced fund-raiser, these newcomers are encouraged to sell candy, flowers, or simply to beg for gifts for their cause.

Because the Unification Church has over 100 front organizations, the names they use often vary. They may say they are raising funds to help Christian young people, or they may mention the name of an organization that has the word *new* or *challenge* in its title. Titles are often chosen to be attractive to people in a given situation.

Because people have grown wise to their tactics, many Moonies have resorted to lies. When the trainers are asked if they represent the Unification Church or Rev. Moon, many will deny it. Later they will justify this to their trainees as "heavenly deception." They claim this is alright, since they are only trying to get back from Satan (those who don't believe as they do) what is rightfully God's.

New recruits to the Unification Church cannot comprehend that they are using the same deceptive tactics that were used to falsely recruit them. Their minds have been controlled by a rote repetition of thoughts, words, and actions. They have been *brainwashed;* their own thoughts have been replaced with the thoughts and commands of someone else.

What encouragement do you get from Jesus in Mark 1:17 and John 8:31–32? What claim did Jesus predict in Matthew 7:21–22?

THE MOON IS NOT THE SON!

It is clear that by following Moon a person is going down the wrong street. In fact, it is a dead-end street. Only by faith in Jesus Christ can we be saved. And only by demonstrating His love to those around us can we truly serve Him. Moon is not the Son. Only Jesus is God's Son, who came and lived a perfect life and died a perfect death so that we might have perfect peace with Him forever **(Matthew 20:28).**

REMEMBER

Be faithful, even to the point of death, and I will give you the crown of life.

Revelation 2:10

FOR NEXT TIME

How many different cults can you name that have their roots in the Eastern, contemplative religions, such as Hinduism or Buddhism? What do you know about these religions?

Session 30

The New Light from the East Is Dark!

"WISE MEN FROM THE EAST"

The modern cult known as Hare Krishna, or the International Society of Krishna Consciousness, dates back to the 15th century, when a Hindu teacher developed the doctrines of Krishnaism from the Hindu god Vishnu. You learned in session 4 that Hindus talk about three main gods: Brahma, the creator; Vishnu, the sustainer; and Siva, the destroyer. Hindus believed that their gods often show themselves in many different forms. One such branch of Hinduism, called Vishnuism, said that the god Vishnu had shown himself as the god Krishna.

A teacher named Chaitanya Mahaprabhu taught that Krishna was actually the god who had revealed himself as Vishnu. This made Krishna preeminent and, therefore, more important. Chaitanya was trying to make Hinduism appealing to more people. Christianity had become popular, so, in competition, Hindus sought to make their gods more personal and approachable.

In 1965 Krishnaism came to America in the person of Abhay Charan De Bhaktivedanta Swami Prabhupada. He advanced the worship of Krishna and founded the International Society of Krishna Consciousness. He remained its leader until his death in 1978. Since then, Hare Krishna has been led by two separate governing bodies, one overseeing the spiritual matters and another the physical administrative needs of the group.

The beliefs of this Hindu sect cause Christians to announce that it is totally incompatible with the teachings of Jesus Christ as recorded in the Holy Scriptures. Even a cursory examination of each uncovers irreconcilable differences.

HARE KRISHNA LIFE-STYLE

Hare Krishna devotees have come to be well known by their saffron robes, shaved heads, and chants of "Hare Krishna." Devotees often frequent airports and public streets, begging or offering to trade their literature for gifts of money.

Four basic rules govern the conduct of all new devotees: no gambling, no intoxicants, no illicit sex, and no eating of meat, fish, or eggs. In addition, new devotees are taught to chant, to participate in temple rituals, and to lie flat in front of their statues of marble and wood.

After recruits have participated in temple ceremonies for six months, they are eligible for the ceremony of initiation. A special fire-ceremony involves the giving of a new holy name and burning several grains on top of a fire built in the center of the temple room reserved for this ceremony. They are then given strands of neck beads, often called the Krishna "dog collar."

After another six months the devotee is eligible for a second ceremony, the brahminical initiation. They are then considered to be brahmin—special people. For men this ceremony involves conferring a sacred thread to be worn over the left shoulder and chest. They are then given a special mantra, or chant, which they are to repeat three times daily.

The next step up the ladder of Krishnaism is *sannyasa,* or renunciation. This involves a lifelong vow of poverty and celibacy and a commitment to preach and do good works. When encountering someone who has reached this state, other Hare Krishna members are to lie flat on the floor before them, indicating their reverence.

Ultimately, Hare Krishnas hope to spend their entire lives in loving service to Krishna. This, known as *bhakti,* teaches that such loving service to God is the only path to truth and happiness. They are taught that only in this stage can people sow good works and build credits in their spiritual bank account.

Chanting is an extremely important aspect of Hare Krishna. Devotees are told to repeat a particular mantra, or Sanskrit word, over and over. This word, given only to them, becomes the key whereby they unlock their entrance into god-conciousness. As they empty their minds of all other thoughts, Hare Krishnas are told, they can please their god.

Read Matthew 12:43–45; Colossians 3:12; and Philippians 4:8. What do they say about our life-style and worship?

BELIEFS OF HARE KRISHNA

Belief in God

Like Hindus, Hare Krishnas believe that there is no way in which they can know their god. Actually, they believe that God is no different from the creation that He began. As a result, Hare Krishnas have few certainties. As an impersonal nonentity, God is unapproachable. No one can ever know if his or her efforts of service are acceptable—or even if they are ever heard and recognized.

Compare these beliefs with Matthew 4:10; 9:13; and Psalm 51:16–17.

Attitude toward Jesus Christ

According to Hare Krishna teachings, Jesus is merely another one of Krishna's sons. Like all cults, Hare Krishna denies the essential nature of Jesus Christ. Thus, they have cut themselves off from any hope of forgiveness or the assurance of eternal life with God. With their denial of Jesus, they also deny the only source of forgiveness. Since they also deny the basic sinfulness of all people, they do not realize the calamity of their error.

Salvation for the Hare Krishna consists of chanting enough rounds on their beads and offering enough good works to their god.

Devotees of Hare Krishna have no faith in a Savior, but rather in an enlightened guru, or teacher, who presents the proper *way*.

Tell how each of the following passages shows the fallacy of a Hare Krishna belief: 1 John 5:20; Romans 3:23; Ephesians 2:8–10; 4:4–6.

Krishna Scriptures

Hare Krishna devotees respect all Hindu scriptures, but place special significance on the *Bhagavad-Gita,* as translated into English by their founder, Prabhupada. They also believe that the International Society of Krishna Conciousness magazine, *Back to the Godhead,* is the only true interpretation of their scriptures.

How do you react to this quote from *Back to the Godhead?* "Everything we've thought or done during our life makes an impression on our mind, and the sum total of all these impressions determines our final thoughts at death. According to the quality of these thoughts, we are awarded a suitable new body after death" (*Back to the Godhead,* Vol. 11, No. 1).

Afterlife in Hare Krishna

Like the Hindu religion, Hare Krishna believes in reincarnation. As can be seen from the previous quote from *Back to the Godhead,* the state of one's afterlife is determined by one's thoughts immediately before death. Not only is this scary, but it offers no comfort whatsoever.

Compare these beliefs with Scripture. See, for example, Romans 5:8; Hebrews 9:27; 9:12, 28; 1 Peter 3:18; and John 3:16–17.

WITNESSING TO A HARE KRISHNA

Obviously it will be very difficult to witness your faith to a Hare Krishna. Words and concepts are different. There is the barrier of differing thought patterns. But finally, we must share our faith with anyone who asks **(1 Peter 3:15).** Perhaps a Hare Krishna you encounter won't specifically ask you about your beliefs. But as opportunities present themselves, share the certainty of your faith in Jesus. Point them to the free grace of Jesus, who died that we might live. Even though they may not be aware of it, remind them that everyone is guilty of sin. Point them to the blood of Jesus, which cleanses them from all sin **(1 John 1:7–9).**

Eastern religions claim to bring light to people in the West, whereas they really offer only more darkness, which, when added to the darkness of sin already there, leaves people in a hopeless condition. Prepare yourself to make a simple witness to your faith in Jesus. When you have a chance, point people to Jesus, who died that all might live! Remember, God loves the whole world **(John 3:16)!**

REMEMBER

The god of this age has blinded the minds of unbelievers, so that they cannot see the light of the gospel of the glory of Christ, who is the image of God.

2 Corinthians 4:4

FOR NEXT TIME

You have probably heard of a religion called Christian Science. How many other "Science" religions you can name?

Session 31

New Science Religions

CHRISTIAN SCIENCE

Mary Baker Eddy

Mary Baker Eddy, founder of the Church of Christ, Scientist, was born in New Hampshire in 1821. From the beginning, she was not healthy, struggling with numerous ailments, ranging from paralysis to hysteria to poor eyesight.

After the death of her first husband, Mary began to dabble in the occult. She became interested in contacting the dead, conducted several seances, and read widely on the subject of spiritualism.

In 1862 Mary met Phineas P. Quimby, a healer who called himself a doctor. She claims she fell asleep while he was rubbing her head, and when she awoke, she was completely healed of all her infirmities. Quimby claimed to have discovered that the secrets of Christ's healing powers were basically mind control! Mary immediately became his devoted disciple, dedicating her life to preaching Quimby's *gospel of salvation,* which may have amounted to a little dose of psychology and a big dose of mesmerism, or *stroking with magnets.*

In 1866, less than a month after Quimby's death, Mary discovered Christian Science and hardly referred to Quimby again. She claimed that an immediate recovery from an injury that neither medicine nor surgery could reach led her to discover how to be well herself, and how to make others so.

In 1875 Mary published *Science and Health with Key to the Scriptures.* Members of Christian Science congregations throughout the world use this standard guide at worship and private devotions.

The church itself was chartered on July 4, 1876, with the first congregation founded three years later. Mary lived until 1910. Christian Scientists claimed that MAM (Malicious Animal Magnetism—mental persecution from her enemies) took her life.

Christian Science Popularized

The church grew quite rapidly. Some have suggested that most of the church's 100,000 members are middle-aged or elderly women in the more affluent areas of the country. Actually, those who seek the healing offered by the church seem to outnumber the members of the church themselves.

Mrs. Eddy began to teach her art of healing at the Massachusetts Metaphysical College in 1881. The sole faculty at this school, she charged $300 for 12 lessons. As a result of her writing and teaching, Mrs. Eddy amassed a fortune estimated in excess of two million dollars.

Toward the end of her life, Mary Baker Eddy moved several times, each time to avoid the dreaded MAM which, she said, had claimed the life of her third husband. During a deathbed conversation with her trusted associate, Dickey, Mary reportedly said, "If I should ever leave here, will you promise me that you will say that I was mentally murdered?" Dickey replied, "Yes, Mother."

Christian Science, the Bible and Christ

Mrs. Eddy claimed most emphatically that the source of her theological system was the Holy Bible. In *Science and Health,* p. viii, she says, "The Bible was [my] sole teacher." Her writings, however, show that although the Scriptures were *her* guide, she directed others to her *Key to the Scriptures,* beginning on page 499 of her book, rather than to the Bible itself. Her interpretation of the Bible is placed above that of the Holy Spirit, working through the Word itself! Rather than opening the Scriptures, her so-called *key* obscures them.

Mrs. Eddy contends that God is All; He is not a material being, He is Mind. If God is All and God is Mind, all that *really* exists must be mind or spirit. Matter cannot exist if all is mind, since mind is not matter. Not only so, but God is good; if God is good and *all* is good, evil (which includes sin, sickness, and death) cannot *really* exist. Such things seem to exist only because we refuse to recognize that God is All.

Furthermore, Christian Science states that humans are not matter—mortal existence is a dream. Sin and mortality have not actual origin or rightful existence, and death is but a mortal illusion, an *error,* or false idea.

Lamb of God no longer refers to Jesus Christ, but to a spiritual idea of love.

Since people aren't sinful, Mrs. Eddy saw no reason for belief in Christ's atoning death on the cross. In fact, Jesus was no more than *the first practitioner of Christian Science.* His suffering and death are meaningless to us today, since these facts are simply history.

Write a response to the Christian Science philosophy. What does the Bible teach about the human condition and about Christ? How would you witness to Christian Science members?

SCIENTOLOGY

Beginnings: L. Ron Hubbard

L. Ronald Hubbard, the son of an officer in the U. S. Navy, was born in Nebraska in 1911. He traveled extensively, especially in Asia. During these travels he became acquainted with such Eastern religions as Hinduism and Buddhism.

According to his own accounts, Hubbard studied science and mathematics at George Washington University and later received his Ph.D. from Princeton. It is said that before World War II he had published over 15 million words in books and articles. His greatest success seemed to be in science fiction novels.

During the war he was a commander, and was extensively decorated. By the end of the war he was crippled and blinded, so he resumed his studies of philosophy. He claims that discoveries he made allowed him to return to full combat duty within three years. Others disagree about his educational and combat records.

Dianetics

Hubbard said that between 1923 and 1953 he received numerous "cosmological revelations," which ultimately allowed him to publish his most famous work, *Dianetics: The Modern Science of Mental Health* (Hubbard, 1950). The term *dianetics,* Hubbard explains, comes from Greek words meaning "through" and "soul." The idea of dianetics is to be "through the soul" or "through thoughts."

Scientology Popularized

As a result of the success of his book, Hubbard opened a series of clinics or Dianetics processing centers. Hubbard founded the Church of Scientology and took advantage of various tax benefits offered to churches. He also sought the First Amendment freedom of speech and religion.

Many who have witnessed the phenomenal growth of Scientology recall a somewhat prophetic statement made by Hubbard in the late 1940s, "Writing for a penny a word is ridiculous. If a man wants to make a million dollars, the best way would be to start his own religion" (quoted by Frederick R. Harm in *How to Respond to the Science Religions* [Concordia, 1981, p. 37]). Hubbard did start his own religion, and has grown rich from its profits.

Scientology, the Bible and Christ

Scientology actually makes no comments about the Bible. Rather, the writings of Hubbard make up the Scientology "bible."Thus, Scientologists make Hubbard a new Savior who replaces Jesus Christ. Since people are not sinful, they need no Savior from sin. According to Hubbard, people are incapable of error.

Develop a response to Scientology. How does it differ from your response to the Christian Scientists?

REMEMBER

If God is for us, who can be against us? He who did not spare His own Son, but gave Him up for us all—how will He not also, along with Him, graciously give us all things?

Romans 8:31–32

FOR NEXT TIME

Write what you think the terms *mind control, brainwashing,* and *deprogramming* mean, and describe your attitudes toward them. Although it may be rather difficult, imagine that you are a parent. You have just received a phone call informing you that your son or daughter has joined a religious cult. Describe your reactions. What, if anything, do you think you would do?

Session 32

Entering and Leaving Cults

CONVERSION

If anyone is in Christ, he is a new creation; the old has gone, the new has come! All this is from God, who reconciled us to Himself through Christ and gave us the ministry of reconciliation: that God was reconciling the world to Himself in Christ, not counting men's sins against them.

2 Corinthians 5:17–19

This passage illustrates one important aspect of entering cults—conversion. Conversion occurs when Christ enters a person's heart and this person believes. This happens instantaneously, either during infant baptism or through God's Word later in life. The Holy Spirit enters our heart and a new person in Christ arises to walk in a new life with Him **(Romans 6:4)**.

Those within cults would argue, though, that conversion is a process that takes place over a period of time. They use passages like **Romans 12:2: "Do not conform any longer to the pattern of this world, but be transformed by the renewing of your mind."**

The context of this passage, however, shows that Paul is speaking about *sanctification,* the new life we live as God's children. Growth in sanctification *is* a gradual process, one that continues throughout our lives. Conversion, however, occurs instantaneously.

Thus, *our beliefs determine our behavior.* Cult leaders, however, apply just the opposite principle—that behavior determines belief. To gain a recruit they will focus on desirable behavior such as showing kindness to poor people. The recruits may become intensely involved in works of goodness without giving any attention to the beliefs of the cult until "it's too late"—because they have become mindless zombies who follow leaders and ideologies that they otherwise would never even have thought of following!

HOW WOULD YOU REACT?

Imagine you are the parent of a young person seduced into a cult in a scenario similar to the one described in session 29. Your daughter or son is invited to a free dinner/informational meeting. This meeting is quickly followed by a very attractive-sounding weekend retreat, which is also followed by a week- or monthlong field trip.

This field trip turns out to be a cult indoctrination camp in which certain authority and controls are placed over new recruits, so that when the camp is over, they don't want to return home. They are instead taught that total allegiance is to be offered to the cult leader, and since family and former friends will only try to remove them from *this wonderful setting,* they are warned against further contact with them. They are, in fact, encouraged to write or phone these *former* associates and formally renounce all connection with their former way of life.

As a parent who is the recipient of such a letter or call, how would you react? Would you be angry? scared? What if you repeatedly tried to recontact your child, only to reach a dead end? How would you then react? Would you be interested in contacting some *deprogrammers.* For a sum of money these people would kidnap your young person from the cult and spend a great deal of time and effort to return this person to his or her former state of mental being.

SHOULD DEPROGRAMMING BE ILLEGAL?

Even though cult deprogramming is illegal, with fines and even jail sentences facing those who are caught, many cult deprogrammers continue to operate in the U. S., although they cannot be found in the yellow pages of your telephone directory.Cultic experts don't agree on the use of coercive tactics to help people get out of cults. Several things are certain, however. Left to their own devices and the equally coercive tactics used to maintain cult membership, few young people simply walk out of a cult. And if they do, they may encounter even greater problems later.

Unfortunately, most deprogrammers treat the exiting cult member psychologically and sociologically, but few deal with the *spiritual* needs of these people. Many departing cult members develop an unhealthy negative attitude toward any religious institution, Christian or cultic. They often feel, "once bitten, twice shy!"

WHO IS VULNERABLE TO CULTS?

Cults focus their recruitment efforts primarily on people who "face a change" in their lives, perhaps being called on for the first time to make an adult decision. This could happen, for example, when someone

- enters college;
- finishes college;
- moves away from old friends;
- experiences the divorce or death of a parent; or
- receives a new brother or sister.

Many cult recruits are "loners." *Many others, however, are "doers"* — individuals who are very idealistic and socially involved. Cult recruitment is definitely not limited to one group of persons (thought there is a focus on people 17 to 25 years old).

CULTIC MANIPULATION

Following extensive interviews with American servicemen who were prisoners of the Chinese during the Korean War, Robert J. Lifton and others have suggested that the techniques (often called *brainwashing*) used on the POWs are strikingly similar to those used by cults. Briefly, these are

1. control of environment and time—extreme structure;
2. manipulation of the environment—frenzy of activity, no chance to check out reality;
3. guilt producing—frequent confessional sessions, everything past is bad;
4. deprivation and abuse—deprive of sleep, protein, privacy, medical attention, possessions (including money);
5. stripping of identity—especially of adult status;
6. control of language—words take on new meaning;
7. ideology over reality—whatever disagrees with the group isn't real;
8. thought-stopping—through chanting, or meditating;
9. total denial of self—transfer allegiance to a human leader.

RESULTANT BEHAVIOR

Former cult members have described and displayed behaviors that are also similar to *brainwashed* POWs. These include

1. constant guilt and self-criticism;
2. adopting goals often far below the individual's ability;
3. strong hostility toward former environment and associates;

4. total dependency on a human master;
5. rapid and complete reorientation of life;
6. frequent and unexplained lapses into trancelike state.

Regardless of whether or not you agree that cult members have been brainwashed, these behaviors indicate a strong control of one group over another.

Notice how St. Paul reacted to such behavior in his day: **"There are many rebellious people, mere talkers and deceivers, especially those of the circumcision group. They must be silenced, because they are ruining whole households by teaching things they ought not to teach—and that for the sake of dishonest gain"** (Titus 1:10–11).

"LEAVE THEM ALONE AND THEY'LL COME HOME!"

That was the advice to Little Bo-Peep in the nursery rhyme. Does the same apply to members of cults? Hardly, though such an alternative would prevent another bad (worse?) approach—nagging!

One former member of Moon's Unification Church said, "My mother loved me out." She argued vigorously with her son when he first joined the cult, but then she maintained a long period of loving, nonjudgmental communication. When the son was punished one day for not meeting his fund-raising quota for the cult, he realized that he saw Jesus' unconditional love mirrored in his mother (while love within the cult was conditional)! Unknowingly, the mother had followed these suggestions:

1. Let the new cultist know where you stand.
2. Don't argue with the person.
3. Nurture valid doubts and misgivings about the cult.
4. Bide your time.
5. Remain sensitive to signs that your help is wanted.
6. Continue to affirm love for and commitment to the loved one.

REMEMBER

The Spirit clearly says that in later times some will abandon the faith and follow deceiving spirits and things taught by demons. Such teachings come through hypocritical liars, whose consciences have been seared as with a hot iron. . . . Have nothing to do with godless myths and old wives' tales; rather, train yourself to be godly. For physical training is of some value, but godliness has value for all things, holding promise for both the present life and the life to come.
1 Timothy 4:1–2, 7–8

Session 33

Review of Sessions 28–32

Give brief, yet complete, answers to the following questions.

1. Name the 1960s and 1970s movement on which the new Christian cults "piggybacked."

2. Describe this movement and the reasons it grew and flourished.

3. How do cults require recruits to make sacrifices?

4. Compare the goal of most "New Christian" cults with the goals of Christian Churches.

5. Describe the group known as the Children of God.

6. Briefly describe the founding of the Unification Church.

7. How do Moon's teachings regard the Bible?

8. How does Moon regard the life and work of Jesus?

9. Briefly describe the main teachings of Eastern religions.

10. Describe life in the Hare Krishna.

11. Describe the training received by new Hare Krishna members.

12. How does Hare Krishna regard the Bible and Jesus Christ?

13. How do Eastern religions deal with the concept of an afterlife?

14. Who were Mary Baker Eddy and Phineas P. Quimby, and how did each contribute to the founding of the Church of Christ, Scientist?

15. What group of people are particularly attracted to Christian Science, and what has contributed to the popularity of this group?

16. What did L. Ron Hubbard do before he founded the Church of Scientology?

17. How do Christian Science and Scientology differ in their attitudes toward the Bible and Jesus Christ?

18. How could you best witness to people involved in one of the Science religions?

19. How can people's minds be controlled?

20. Why is the topic of deprogramming so controversial?

21. Describe several characteristics that make young people vulnerable to cultic recruitment.

22. Give several examples of techniques used by cults to manipulate people in the groups.

23. Describe characteristic behavior for cult members.

24. Tell how you would witness to a cult member.

UNIT 6

Satanic Cults

An explosion of satanic and occult activity has occurred in the past two decades, particularly in the United States. Movies and books have done much to popularize these activities. But the real reason for the increase is Satan himself.

He is a very clever promoter. Since the beginning he has been seeking ways to lead people away from God **(Genesis 3:1–7).** Satan even attacked our Lord Jesus Himself **(Matthew 4:1–11).** Is it any wonder that he would also try to turn us away from God?

This unit could be quite controversial. Committed Christians "innocently" practice some of the activities identified as *occult*. But we must listen to and heed what God has said in His revealed Word. Satan would love to have us dismiss the rightful condemnation of something we think is harmless.

If God has spoken, we must listen. Failing to listen, we risk going down the path that leads to destruction **(Matthew 7:13).** Too many young people have begun to walk that path and found that when they tried to "turn around," they were unable to do so!

Some cults simply *use* occult practices as entertainment. But many highly organized cults focus all their attention on Satan and the power he can give them.

As you study this unit, you may become frightened at what you read and discuss. Remember: **"The one who is in you is greater than the one who is in the world" (1 John 4:4).** That One is Jesus. Never forget that He lives *in* you. He continues to hold you tightly in His grasp. Bask in His peace, knowing that He holds you!

Session 34

Satan Is "Alive and Well": The Occult Explosion

OCCULT EXPLOSION

The root word for *occult* means *secret* or *hidden*. By itself, it refers to activities that heretofore were unfamiliar and even hidden from public view. A rapid increase of satanic activity in our world has catapulted the demonic into everyone's view and attracted an increasing number of average American people.

"Satan himself masquerades as an angel of light" (2 Corinthians 11:14). Although Satan is invisible, evidences of his increased activity in our world are not. You can find a few references to organized satanic activity in most daily newspapers, and invisible, implied evidences of Satan's presence are everywhere. **What are some ways in which Satan masquerades, or passes himself off as being good, in our world today?**

Children's books, TV, and toys fascinate kids with magic spells, protective charms, love potions, and mysterious force fields. They suggest very subtly that there is a supernatural force, other than God, to which people can and should turn for help.

As they grow older, young people are exposed to more sophisticated but equally deceitful devices of the devil. They become enamored with the music of their favorite rock stars and emulate the life-style of these heroes, often becoming involved in drugs, sex, and satanic rituals, which are also graphically illustrated in videos. This music pounds the devilish themes into their heads for hours each day.

Many adults think they are more mature and therefore immune to such lies, but they are not. Newspapers carry seemingly harmless astrological columns. Millions receive their advice with varying degrees of acceptance. Popular soap operas that monopolize TV feature thinly disguised but definitely satanic perversions of marriage, sexuality, and family life. The gods of consumerism are worshiped in retail outlets across the country and are praised in all forms of advertising. They fuel the sinful desires everyone has to *have it all* now.

Satan is working overtime to lead God's faithful people to the foot of the altar of self-worship. Having accomplished this, Satan can easily place himself on the throne of peoples' hearts.

1. Why, do you think, has there been greatly increased activity by the Evil Foe in our world today?

2. How have Christians been fighting against this satanic onslaught?

3. What confidence do the words of **1 John 3:8** give you?

4. Why is it important for Christians to become informed about Satan?

KNOW YOUR ENEMY *AND* HIS STRATEGY

From the Scriptures below find the names of the wicked enemy of Christians, as well as military terminology that describes the struggle in which we are engaged. These names are also hidden in the Word Find.

1. Struggle or contest in which Christians are involved **(2 Timothy 4:7).**

2. Protective equipment available to every believer **(Ephesians 6:11).**

3. Weapon given to Christians **(Ephesians 6:17).**

4. Projectiles used by Satan to attack Christians **(Ephesians 6:16).**

5. Name for the Evil Foe; means deceiver, or liar **(John 8:44).**

6. Another name for the Evil Foe; means adversary, or opponent **(Matthew 12:26).**

S	Z	U	A	R	R	0	W	S
H	S	T	C	N	W	D	T	T
B	G	V	A	X	R	R	T	G
N	L	T	E	0	A	D	A	P
T	A	F	W	D	R	Q	L	N
S	C	S	I	O	F	I	E	E
F	R	N	M	G	V	P	C	T
L	F	R	T	E	H	A	J	K
J	A	G	D	D	R	T	Z	Y

WHY AN OCCULT EXPLOSION?

Many factors have fueled interest in the occult in recent years. The *drug cult* has certainly contributed to an increased interest in the unknown. Popular movies that depicted satanic activity also have helped to interest people in obscure, demonic activity.

Furthermore, people are anxious and curious about many things, especially their future. When peoples' lives are filled with doubt and uncertainty, they often grasp at anything for security. They may be intrigued by suggestions that horoscopes and Ouija boards can predict their future. Occult powers offer a tangible reality to people who may suffer from weakened faith in a God who doesn't show Himself visibly. Occult power is real. It works! It offers the involvement that church people often crave.

Finally, the explosion of occult activity and interest is a sign of the times (**Mark 13:22; 1 Timothy 4:1**). As the end of the world approaches, Satan, knowing that his time is short, will work that much harder, frantically trying to drag more of God's followers down to hell with him.

WHAT IS YOUR ATTITUDE?

In *Responding to the Occult* (Concordia, 1977, pages 10–11) Rev. David Hoover has suggested that there are several attitudes people have adopted toward things of the Occult.

(a) "These influences . . . are inevitable. They are here to stay, and there is nothing to worry about."

(b) "This interest . . . is only a fad. Wait awhile and it will go away."

(c) " . . . we should shut our eyes and ears, bury our heads, and, probably, communicate nothing."

(d) "It is all highly intriguing and we should learn as much as possible, even by dabbling a little ourselves."

1. What do you think about these four different attitudes? What fallacy can you find in each one?

2. Write a description of your own attitude. Tell how you feel about occult activities and beliefs.

3. Compare your ideas with the four listed above.

WHAT DOES THE BIBLE SAY ABOUT SATAN?

1. Read **Ephesians 6:11–18**. Why is Satan so dangerous? Is it because he is stronger than God? Or is he perhaps able to catch you unawares? As people who hope to stand against him, what do we desperately need? Where do we get it? Most of the things described in this section are defensive, pieces of a suit of armor. How can each piece help you stand against Satan?

What is the only thing we can use to actually attack Satan? What does this tell you about doing battle with Satan by yourself?

2. Read **1 Peter 5:8–9**. What does Satan want to do with you? Explain Peter's (and God's) suggestions for fighting against Satan.

3. Read the account of the encounter of Paul and Barnabas with the Jewish false prophet Bar-Jesus in **Acts 13:6–12**. (He was also called Elymas and was a sorcerer.) Identify characteristics of people who oppose God. Also consider **Mark 5:1–13** as you create your list.

Satan is very tricky. He means to destroy anything that Christ or His followers do. In Jesus' own estimation, Satan is a liar, a murderer, and has been that way from the beginning (**John 8:44**). He means no good!

4. Now go back to the attitude you described in No. 2 of the preceding section. Do you still feel the same way about Satan and his occult activities? Perhaps you wish to change or add to what you have written. Remember, Satan is no fool. Jesus Christ, however, is stronger than Satan. When we are armed with Jesus Christ, Satan can successfully be resisted.

THREE MAJOR CATEGORIES

We shall look at three major categories of the occult during this unit:

(1) Astrology or fortune-telling—session 35

(2) Magick—session 36

(3) Spiritism—session 37

REMEMBER

Having disarmed the powers and authorities, He [God the Father] made a public spectacle of them, triumphing over them by the cross.

Colossians 2:15

Since the children have flesh and blood, He too shared in their humanity so that by His death He might destroy him who holds the power of death—that is, the devil—and free those who all their lives were held in slavery by their fear of death.

Hebrews 2:14–15

FOR NEXT TIME

We will be talking about astrology and fortune-telling. We have already mentioned horoscopes. See how many other forms of fortune-telling you can list.

Session 35

Astrology: It's in the Stars

GOD IS NOT SILENT ABOUT ASTROLOGY

When you look up to the sky and see the sun, the moon and the stars—all the heavenly array—do not be enticed into bowing down to them and worshiping things the Lord your God has apportioned to all the nations under heaven. But as for you, the Lord took you and brought you out of the iron-smelting furnace, out of Egypt, to be the people of his inheritance, as you now are.

Deuteronomy 4:19–20

ASTROLOGY ORIGINATED FROM ASTRONOMY

One familiar form of fortune-telling is astrology. The word "astrology" comes from two other words, "astra," which means star, and "logos," which means word or study about. Astrology in its obsolete sense means astronomy, the science of the stars. In its present sense astrology encourages the belief that the heavenly bodies control events and human character.

Certain inanimate objects such as the seas and oceans *do* change with the position of the moon. Powerful tides silently testify to this great power. This can be demonstrated and proven scientifically. But there is no basis in fact for the belief that the positioning of the stars at the birth of a person has anything to do with the character or future of that person.

Furthermore, astrology is based on "signs" or constellations, formed by various stars. These are nothing more than imaginative "star pictures" the ancients thought the stars formed. Against the backgrown of these 12 astrological signs move the five planets known to ancient man, and also the sun and the moon. Three additional planets have been discovered since the Zo-

diac was developed by the ancient Persians! Furthermore, *precession,* the slow wobble of the earth's axis, makes it necessary to revise star charts periodically, so the dates given in horoscopes no longer correspond with the daily position of the sun in the sky in modern times!

Thus, when people took a "logical" step from a belief that the moon controlled the tides to a belief that history was predetermined by the stars, they took a leap that passes the test of neither science nor Scripture.

A CHRISTIAN ATTITUDE TOWARD THE FUTURE

While we reject the attempts to use astrology to predict the future, we can rejoice that God has a plan for our lives and is actively working to carry it out. The greatest part of that plan was revealed in Jesus Christ. God's great love for us was demonstrated in Christ's selfless suffering and dying on the cross. God proved that *all* of His plans and promises will come to pass. He proved it by the resurrection of Jesus from the dead. In His inspired Word, the Bible, He has revealed all that we need to know about our future. We can be absolutely certain of the most important part of our future. Through faith in Jesus we know we will be with God forever.

Many people read horoscope columns in their daily newspapers, hoping to find some scrap of information about their future. Actually (and happily), our futures are in God's hands. He doesn't want us to know more about our future than He has already revealed to us in Holy Scriptures. Many of us know what we *hope* will happen in our futures. But what has God told you in His truth, the Word of God? **Write about your own future. Be sure to include Bible verses that describe your future with certainty.**

ASTROLOGY IS IDOLATRY

It is a sad day when people transfer the worship and praise due their Creator, to objects that He has created. Astrology and related fortune-telling practices are actually idolatry. God condemns idolatry in the First Commandment **(Exodus 20:1–6).** He also condemns astrology. Reread **Deuteronomy 4:19–20** printed at the beginning of this session. In **Isaiah 47:13–15** God also reveals the folly of heeding the advice of astrologers. Not only can they not save us, but in the end they will be judged for their idolatry and will be burned up!

In what ways could reading a horoscope or visiting a crystal ball gazer be idolatry? Would it be wrong to read the fortunes contained in Chinese fortune cookies? Talk about it.

WHAT HAPPENS TO THOSE WHO GET INVOLVED?

Christian counselors have helped free people from their enslavement to astrology and fortune-telling. Many agree that while the results of these practices may at first appear attractive, in the long run they are devastating and frequently faith-threatening! Since Satan is "the father of lies" **(John 8:44),** you can expect a great deal of *lying* or *deceit* whenever you deal with astrology. People who wish they had occult powers, but don't, often lie in order to convince unsuspecting individuals to follow them.

As sinful humans we are highly *susceptible to suggestion.* Someone may innocently suggest that something will happen to us, and Satan can use this to create doubt in our minds. Some say they only read the daily horoscope out of curiosity. Yet many of these same people confess an occasional hesitancy to continue with certain day-to-day plans when their horoscope has advised against it!

While some fortune-telling is purely fake or suggestion, some astrologers do use such occult devices as crystal balls and tarot cards to make their predictions. Those who object, saying that these are only inanimate objects, must remember that these objects are used in occult practices clearly condemned by God **(Deuteronomy 18:10–14).**

Many who have had repeated or prolonged contact with occult practices later tell of a strong resistance to Christian spiritual things. They report difficulty in prayer and often find it hard, if not impossible, to read the Bible. Many of them also experience a decay in their moral standards.

There are other dangerous effects of astrology and fortune-telling. As a master liar Satan has thoroughly convinced many people of the attractiveness of his power and has won them over. We can only hope that they will see the danger of such involvement and turn to the truth of Jesus' eternal Gospel—before it is too late for them!

CHRISTIAN CONCLUSIONS ABOUT ASTROLOGY AND FORTUNE-TELLING

Having briefly examined the occult world of astrology and fortune-telling, we cannot remain neutral about Satan and his bag of tricks. If we choose to become involved in astrology or fortune-telling itself, we risk damaging or even destroying our faith in Jesus Christ. On the other hand, if we realize the danger of such occult involvement, we also will become concerned about theose who are already involved. God will move us not only to become informed ourselves but also to warn others.

Following are four conclusions about astrology and fortune-telling:

1. Any form of fortune-telling is strictly forbidden by Scripture **(Leviticus 20:6, 27; Deuteronomy 18:10–14; 29:29; 1 Chronicles 10:13; Jeremiah 29:8–9).**

2. Attempts at forecasting the future are always unreliable, unless the source of such information is from God **(Deuteronomy 18:21–22; Matthew 6:25–34; James 1:5).**

3. Fortune-telling is very dangerous **(Matthew 12:30; Leviticus 20:22; 1 Chronicles 10:13; Jeremiah 29:8–9).**

4. God has given promises through Jesus that are far greater and much more wonderful than anything Satan tries to show us through fortune-telling (for example, **John 3:16; Hebrews 13:5b–6; 1 Peter 5:7).**

REMEMBER

Then the lawless one will be revealed, whom the Lord Jesus will overthrow with the breath of His mouth and destroy by the splendor of His coming. The coming of the lawless one will be in accordance with the work of Satan, displayed in all kinds of counterfeit miracles, signs and wonders, and in every sort of evil that deceives those who are perishing. They perish because they refused to love the truth and so be saved.

2 Thessalonians 2:8–10

FOR NEXT TIME

What's the difference between the popular form of entertainment, called "stage magic" or "slight of hand," and the magick (or black magic) in which the practitioner resorts to occult objects or rituals?

Session 36

Witchcraft and Magick

WHAT'S THE DIFFERENCE?

Have you ever watched popcorn pop? Its like magic! One moment the little kernel is lying quietly in the bottom of the popper, and suddenly it expands and flies wildly about!

Perhaps you have also spent some enjoyable moments watching a magician perform many intriguing tricks. Magic is unbelievable!

1. What is "magic"? Write a definition of the word.

Now look at our definition of the word we spell m-a-g-i-c-k. *Magick is the art of (or at least the attempt at) knowing or ruling the spirit, human, animal, and plant worlds, together with the world of dead matter, through extrasensory means with the aid of the mystical and accompanying ceremonies.*

What does God say about magick? **"Let no one be found among you who sacrifices his son or daughter in the fire, who practices divination or sorcery, interprets omens, engages in witchcraft, or casts spells, or who is a medium or spiritist or who consults the dead. Anyone who does these things is detestable to the Lord, and because of these detestable practices the Lord your God will drive out those nations before you"** (Deuteronomy 18:10–12).

2. Is God amused by *any* kind of magic? Might He be entertained by good stage magic, and yet very, very disappointed by occult magick? What's the difference?

As you look at the Scriptural descriptions of magick and witchcraft in this session, try to develop guidelines to help you judge between harmless stage magic and very dangerous occult magick.

THE BIBLE CONDEMNS MAGICK AND THOSE WHO PRACTICE IT!

When God led His people out of Egypt and toward the Promised Land, He often warned them of the dangers of sorcery and witchcraft. They were told to drive out and destroy the inhabitants of their new land, because so many of the natives practiced sorcery in their religious ceremonies.

But some of the children of Israel also practiced witchcraft! Having lived for so long in Egypt, the children of Israel apparently had picked up some of the idolatrous habits of the Egyptians, including sorcery.

The Greek word for *sorcery* is derived from the same word as *pharmacy*. A sorcerer originally was *one who gave potions*. An older word for sorcerer, *magician*, comes from a Hebrew word that means *one who draws magical lines or circles*. This could be a *horoscopist*, one who conjures up spirits through the use of symbols drawn on the ground.

In giving the First Commandment (**Exodus 20:1–5a**), God acknowledged that He knew that if His people failed to worship Him, they would worship something else. In **22:18** God said, **"Do not allow a sorceress to live."** God condemned the related practices of witchcraft and conjuring up evil spirits (**Deuteronomy 18:10–14**)— spiritism, trying to contact the dead through spirit mediums (**Leviticus 20:27**). These practices often involved burning the sacrifice, including one's own children (**Deuteronomy 18:10**). Our God is a jealous God, and warns against worship of anyone or anything but Him (**Exodus 20:5**).

After they had inhabited their new land for some time, God's people at times adopted some of the evil practices of their new neighbors. God's repeated warnings to His people provide us evidence that this practice was widespread (**1 Samuel 15:23; 2 Kings 17:17; 21:6; 23:24; 1 Chronicles 10:13**).

1. Study these passages. Write a brief statement of what each says.

2. What kind of general statement about God's attitude toward witchcraft and magick can you make? How does God feel about those who practice witchcraft, magick, and divination?

Next we will take a look at how these practices reared their ugly heads in New Testament times.

IF YOU PRACTICE MAGICK, YOU OPPOSE THE KINGDOM OF GOD

Jesus often opposed and drove out wicked powers under the influence of Satan and replaced the evil spirits with His own Holy Spirit. Read about His ministry against Satan in **Matthew 4:1–11, 24** and **8:16, 28–34**. In a classic teaching about Satan, Jesus warned that Satan stood *against* everything that Jesus stood for *(12:22–27)*. No one can remain *neutral* to Jesus, for He said: **"He who is not with Me is against Me"** **(12:30).** If an evil spirit is cast out of a person, and that empty space isn't filled with God's presence, the spirit will undoubtedly return **(12:43–45),** and the final condition of that man is worse than the first!

Paul summed up God's condemnation of evil practices such as practicing magick **(Galatians 5:19–21).** Calling them **"acts of the sinful nature,"** Paul said, **"I warn you, as I did before, that those who live like this will not inherit the kingdom of God."** God does not take occult magick lightly.

The apostles had several encounters with magick. Read one of the following references. Then report to the class on the encounter reported there.

1. **Acts 8:9–24**
2. **Acts 13:6–12**
3. **Acts 16:16–24**
4. **Acts 19:13–20**

LISTEN TO THE LORD'S PROPHET

Several ideas probably emerged during your discussion of the above. Supernatural forces *do* exist. Both good forces (from God) and evil forces (from Satan) are real. This sometimes confuses God's people, since evil supernatural forces do not always identify themselves. Furthermore, Satan often disguises his power, making it look like God's work. As he counterfeits God's loving activity, Satan causes a great deal of confusion.

People seek help from occult sources because they want more knowledge or power. Curiosity often entangles God's people in all sorts of trouble. Sometimes, unwittingly, God's people find that they have sought knowledge or power from the wrong source! God encourages us to turn to Him for knowledge and assistance **(James 1:5; Psalm 50:15)!**

Occult activities prey on the human desire to gain more knowledge or power than God has given us. That's Satan's oldest trick **(Genesis 3:5)!** Furthermore, when people seek more knowledge about their futures, they ignore the fact that secret things belong only to God **(Deuteronomy 29:29).** Also recall that when so-called occult prophets claim to predict the future, they fail the test of God's Word, which clearly states that a true prophet predicts with 100% accuracy **(18:22)!**

Satan is clever, but Christ is all-knowing. Satan deceives us, but Christ always tells us the truth. In His Great Commission **(Matthew 28:18–20)** Jesus tells us to share with the whole world the message of salvation through His grace. He wants more and more people to come to Him, worship Him as the only wise God, and spend an eternity with us praising Him. May you seek knowledge and power from God alone and direct others to Him as well. Wise men still seek Him!

REMEMBER

Jesus said to him, "Away from Me, Satan! For it is written, 'Worship the Lord your God, and serve Him only.' " Then the devil left Him, and angels came and attended Him.

Matthew 4:10–11

I have been crucified with Christ and I no longer live, but Christ lives in me. The life I live in the body, I live by faith in the Son of God, who loved me and gave Himself for me.

Galatians 2:20

FOR NEXT TIME

What is *spiritism* or *spiritualism*? Do you know anyone who is (was) involved in this practice? Have you ever wished that you could contact a dead person? Why would anyone want to?

Session 37

Spiritism: Beyond Death's Door

WHAT HAPPENS AT A SEANCE?

Usually a seance involves people seated around a table, in a darkened room, with some object of focus in the middle. The participants hold hands, and the medium (the "in-between") speaks to and conjures up a spirit. The medium (often called a *transmedium*) speaks to the spirit. This spirit is then designated as their guide in a search for the spirit of a departed friend or loved one with whom they wish to communicate.

The guiding spirit, speaking through the mouth of the medium, generally responds to questions directed to it. The spirit may speak in another voice and claim to be the spirit of a dead person sought by someone in the group. Sometimes the desired spirit is unavailable and the group must be satisfied with communication with the guiding spirit or another more available spirit.

Information given during these sessions is often very general in nature, but sometimes it's quite specific, surprising, and revealing. Occasionally a participant in one of these seances later reports having taken some action at the direction of the medium or guiding spirit. People admit that they became involved in a seance mostly out of curiosity, but some say they genuinely expect to contact the spirit of a dead friend or relative!

Recall your Bible study in the last session. Which passages spoke about spiritism? Can you remember any other verses that speak about contacting the dead?

God gives us a clear prohibition of this practice: **"Do not turn to mediums or seek out spiritists, for you will be defiled by them. I am the Lord your God"** (Leviticus 19:31).

Elsewhere He tells us what we *should* do: **"If any of you lacks wisdom, he should ask God, who gives generously to all without finding fault, and it will be given to him"** (James 1:5).

Some things God in His wisdom knows He must withhold from us: **"The secret things belong to the Lord our God, but the things revealed belong to us and to our children forever, that we may follow all the words of this law"** (Deuteronomy 29:29).

We are not God. We are not all-knowing, nor are we meant to be. If God had wanted us to know every-thing, He would have told us. Even in the garden, in their perfect condition, Adam and Eve didn't know ev-erything. By reserving the tree of the knowledge of good and evil for Himself, God was drawing a simple line between Himself and His people. They were not to be gods! Although we may strongly wish we knew certain things, unless God has revealed them to us, they re-main His secret. To try to tamper with His all-encom-passing knowledge is idolatry.

Let us consider two instances of people who tried to contact the dead.

KING SAUL WANTED TO SPEAK TO THE PROPHET SAMUEL

Read **1 Samuel 28.**

King Saul and David were alienated. Saul was afraid David would take his kingdom. David had sought refuge with the Philistines. As Saul watched the mount-ing forces of the Philistines, he was terrified **(28:5).** Sensing disaster, Saul asked the Lord but received no answer.

Finally, in desperation, Saul ordered his aids to find a medium or sorcerer **(28:7).** This is noteworthy, since he himself had outlawed mediums **(28:3),** as God had commanded **(Deuteronomy 18:9–15; Leviticus 19:26, 31).**

Before he went to the witch at Endor, Saul dis-guised himself, lest the witch would not perform for fear of punishment by the king. Cautiously, the witch warned him when he requested that she conjure up the spirit of the dead Samuel. When Samuel appeared, she re-alized she was dealing with Saul and again expressed her fear of punishment. Calming her fears, Saul asked what she saw.

Since the Bible nowhere indicates that people have the power to communicate with the dead, we do not know whether Saul actually did speak to the spirit of Samuel that day or if it was an evil spirit. In any case, God used the medium in some way to predict his defeat into the hand of the Philistines **(28:16–19)**. (See also the summary of the incident in **1 Chronicles 10:13–14**.) Saul was horrified at the secret information he discovered, wishing he had never sought it.

As we have seen in previous sessions, Satan can counterfeit miracles. Satan has knowledge that is superior to ours, but he is not superior to God's prophets, who can always correctly predict the future. Though Satan may reveal *some* of God's secret things, he is not as powerful as God. He fears Christ **(James 2:19)** and ultimately must flee Christ **(Matthew 4:11)** and all those who belong to Christ **(James 4:7)**.

We must actively resist Satan and all Satanic practices condemned by God. Consider what happened to Saul. He died for his unfaithfulness. Now consider what happened to a modern day religious person.

BISHOP PIKE WANTED TO COMMUNICATE WITH HIS DEAD SON

On Feb. 4, 1966, when his son, James Jr., committed suicide in New York, James Pike Sr. was the Episcopalian bishop for the entire state of California. He was a well-known and respected churchman. The grief and guilt he felt as a result of this incident led Bishop Pike on a rather strange spiritual odyssey that ultimately cost him his life.

Within a few days of his son's death, Pike encountered a number of rather unusual circumstances that reminded him of his son. Repeatedly Pike sought audiences with spiritists who purportedly put him into contact with the spirit of his dead son. Subsequently, this same spirit attempted to relieve him of any guilt or responsibility he felt for the death of his son.

Between the third and fourth of nine seances Pike arranged, a charge of heresy was leveled against him by the Episcopal Church, and he resigned from his office as bishop. During the next three years he intensified his spiritual search. One of his most spectular seances was conducted by medium Arthur Ford, and was broadcast live on Canadian television. At the beginning of the interview Pike conversed with the religion editor of a Toronto newspaper about life after death.

Ford then lapsed into a trance and transmitted several items of information about Pike's son.

Pike also had a number of psychic visions during the three year period after his son's death. The last of these directed him to the desert by the Dead Sea in Israel, where he hoped to make closer contact with his dead son. Pike was later found dead of exposure in the desert. He was some distance from his car.

WHY WOULD ANYONE WANT TO TALK TO THE DEAD?

Review the Scriptural condemnations of spiritism, and the foolishness of such a practice. Why would anyone seek to contact the dead, knowing that God has condemned it so severely? In the Scriptural example, Saul wanted guidance from the dead Samuel. Perhaps some people are simply curious. Pike's interest seems to have centered around his firm belief in a life after death. Apparently he thought such contact with the dead would prove such an afterlife once and for all.

Unfortunately, Pike was not satisfied with the clear promises God has given. He wanted *proof* instead of *faith.* God clearly tells us that whoever believes in His Son has eternal life **(John 3:16)**. Actually, eternal life begins not with death, but when a person believes **(11:25–26)**. Believers will be with Christ forever **(Matthew 28:20)**. This is the main purpose of the Bible— that people may know for sure that they already *have* eternal life **(1 John 5:13)**.

May the Holy Spirit move you, a believer in Jesus as your Lord and Savior, to concentrate your efforts on sharing this certainty with others. May you point others to the certainty of eternal life, based on the revealed Word of God, the Bible, rather than some mystical, Satan-induced plot to redirect their faith.

REMEMBER

Jesus said, . . . "Worship the Lord your God, and serve Him only."

Matthew 4:10

FOR NEXT TIME

We have studied about satanism as it is practiced in our country today. But how organized is it? Since we are talking about other religions in this course, can satanism be properly considered a religion? Write your responses before the next class period.

Session 38

Organized Satanism

SATAN IS ALIVE, ORGANIZED, AND RUNNING OUT OF TIME!

Answer these questions about Satan:

1. Why is he in a hurry to build his kingdom **(Revelation 12:12)?**

2. How does he trick people **(John 8:44)?**

3. What are his goals **(1 Peter 5:8; Matthew 4:9)?**

4. What kind of organization does he have **(Ephesians 6:12; Mark 5:9)?**

5. How can you succeed in your battle with this enemy **(Ephesians 6:13–17)?**

We have looked at many other organized religions and cults. Today we will examine offically organized groups that claim Satan as their head!

SATANISM AND VIOLENT CRIME

You may know about violent crimes committed by people involved in a satanic cult. For example, Charles Manson became infamous when he was implicated with the brutal and ritualistic murders of more than a dozen people, including movie actress Sharon Tate, in Los Angeles in 1969. When he was captured, he spoke to reporters of the girls he had used to commit the murders. "All my women are witches, and I'm the devil," he said (William J. Petersen, *Those Curious Cults in the 80's*, Keats, 1982, page 91).

This is only one example. California alone, in the late 1960s, reported more than 100 murders that were somehow related to the occult.

But organized satanism isn't just recent. In the late 1600s a practice simply called the "Black Mass" scandalized the royal court of Louis XIV of France. One of the king's mistresses, seeking more favor with the king, engaged a person who claimed to have satanic connections. This woman agreed to celebrate a "Black Mass" and provide a love potion. This ceremony required the sacrifice of an infant. This failed, and as she prepared a "Mass of Death" to poison the king, the plot was discovered. The high priestess confessed to having burned over 2,500 infants in the furnace of her house. Their bodies were later discovered by investigators, buried in her garden!

MODERN SATANISM

Modern satanism seems to have begun with Anton Szandor LaVey. LaVey had always been interested in magic. When he became a magician's assistant in a carnival, he began to study the occult in earnest. He read about Aleister Crowley, who had lived in England in the late 19th and early 20th centuries.

Although Crowley couldn't actually be called a satanist, the things he wrote about were satanic. Crowley took great delight in shocking his parents, friends, and especially his very religious uncle, with completely repulsive and unreligious acts. He made a pact with the devil, wrote poems honoring murders, publicly called the Queen dirty names, and played with homosexuality. He encouraged the free use of sex and drugs, and died in a cheap boarding house after daily injecting himself with 11 grams of pure heroin. Crowley taught the simple and complete indulgence of any and all human desires.

LaVey thought Crowley's idea of indulgence quite attractive. He also recognized a great deal of hypocrisy in the church. On Saturday night he would see men lusting after half-naked girls dancing at the carnival. Then on Sunday morning, when he played the organ for tent-show evangelists at the other end of the carnival lot, he would see these same men sitting in the pews with their wives and children, asking God to forgive them and purge them of carnal desires. The next Saturday night they'd be back at the carnival or some other place of indulgence.

He said, "I knew then that the Christian Church thrives on hypocrisy, and that man's carnal nature will out!" He felt that there was need for a church that would recapture people's bodies and their carnal pleasures as objects of celebration. "Since worship of fleshly things produces pleasure," he said, "there would then be a temple of glorious indulgence" (*The Satanic Bible,* Anton LaVey, page 1).

At the end of April 1966 LaVey shaved his head and announced the formation of his Church of Satan. This church would be based on the glorious indulgence of the flesh and would be fun for people. LaVey held Satan as a symbolic personal savior, who takes care of mundane, fleshly, carnal things. LaVey admitted that God exists as a universal force, a balancing factor in nature, but he held that He is too impersonal to care whether we live or die. The devil, LaVey said, deserves a religion that gives him credit. LaVey felt that we should accept without guilt the fact that humans are basically greedy and selfish, sometimes lower than the animals.

LaVey's *Satanic Bible* outsells *The Holy Bible* on many college campuses. Most of the 10,000 members claimed for the Satanic Church are simply recipients of LaVey's monthly newsletter. (Some estimate more than 100,000 people are involved in the satanist movement in the United States.)

Obviously, satanists aren't at all interested in Jesus Christ. In their Black Mass they try to reverse everything they know about Christianity. The cross or crucifix is hung upside down, prayers are prayed backwards, and the altar is covered in black rather than white. Often they seek to have a defrocked priest lead in their worship. They often add sexual rites to make the blasphemy more complete, and sometimes they include animal and even human sacrifices. Apparently some suburban wife-swapping clubs are being converted into satanic covens.

The public creed of LaVey's Church of Satan contains nine statements, including indulgence, vengeance, responsibility only for those who are responsible, the animal nature of man, all the "so-called sins," and the fact that Satan is the best friend the church ever had, since he has kept it in business all these years.

LaVey shuns the spectacular. He forbids drug usage, and denies that he practices the Black Mass. He wishes his church to be just shocking enough to attract people, but not evil enough to attract the wrong kind of attention. His group has undergone many splits because of those who desire more indulgence than LaVey is willing to offer. Perhaps it was just such a group that attracted Comedian Mike Warnke in the late 1960s.

Mike Warnke tells about his experiences with satanism, as well as his exit from that cult and his ensuing life, in *The Satan Seller* (Logos, 1972).

Drugs and sex led to Warnke's entry into satanism. Early "meetings" (more like parties) appealed to him, and at the height of his involvement he presided as a "high priest" at ritual communions at which human blood was drunk and the altar was covered with a naked woman. Sacrifices were commonplace, with some members allowing the last segment of their little finger to be cut off and offered to their Lord, Satan!

Warnke used drugs so heavily that those above him felt he was no longer able to handle the pressures. He was overdosed and dumped, naked, in front of a local hospital. He then tried to run from everything and everyone, including Christians who were constantly dogging him. Fortunately, two roommates shared Jesus Christ with him while he was in a Navy boot camp, and Mike now follows Jesus Christ as his Lord and Savior. Furthermore, he is involved full time in a ministry to help others who have been caught in the web of satanic cults!

CHRIST AND SATAN ARE ENEMIES

1. Think about the teachings of satanism as you saw them in the Crowley, LaVey, and Warnke episodes. Why do you think so many people, especially young people, are attracted to those teachings?

2. God often warns us about people within the church who will try to mislead us—"antichrists," "the man of lawlessness," and the "beast" **(1 John 2:18; 4:3; 2 Thessalonians 2:3–12; Revelation 13:1–10).** Who works through these people **(2 Thessalonians 2:9)?** What does Satan empower them to do **(2:9–10)?** In previous sessions you have seen how Satan has used his guile and power within the province of people who claim to follow God. We should not be surprised by the things we find in a church that openly follows Satan!

3. Many followers of Satan once followed God. On the basis of **Romans 1:21–32** and what you know about satanism, tell what happened to them.

4. Read **Romans 1:16–17.** How alone can you remain faithful to God? What hope can you offer to those who have deserted God for a time?

REMEMBER

[Jesus said,] "My sheep listen to My voice; I know them, and they follow Me. I give them eternal life, and they shall never perish; no one can snatch them out of My hand."

John 10:27–28

[Jesus said,] "Greater love has no one than this, that he lay down his life for his friends."

John 15:13

Contrast Christ's love and promises with Satan's lies!

FOR NEXT TIME

Have you ever heard of the New Age religions or the New Age movement? Between now and the next class period, ask other people. See if they know what the New Age movement is.

Session 39

Unmasking the New Age

IS NEW ALWAYS BETTER?

The time will come when men will not put up with sound doctrine. Instead, to suit their own desires, they will gather around them a great number of teachers to say what their itching ears want to hear. They will turn their ears away from the truth and turn aside to myths. But you, keep your head in all situations, endure hardship, do the work of an evangelist, discharge all duties of your ministry.

2 Timothy 4:3–5

"I AM GOD"

"I am God . . . I am God . . . I am God!"

In January [1987], millions of television viewers heard and saw Shirley MacLaine shout these words to the sea. The scene ended with Ms. MacLaine dissolving in giggles at the utter preposterousness of what she had said. But five hours later, viewers heard the same thought expressed by MacLaine, this time as the "truth" she had learned by having gone Out on a Limb.

During the time between MacLaine's first learning of the New Age movement and her embracing it, viewers were introduced to "trance-channelers," psychics and spirit-guides in the United States, Sweden and Peru. They learned that they are "co-creators" with God, that answers to all questions are to be found in themselves, and that Buddha, Christ and other spiritual leaders were master "politicians." Viewers "soul-traveled" with MacLaine from Peru to the moon via a coiling silver cord and dashed wildly down a winding mountain road in a vehicle steered by an invisible extraterrestrial.

(From "The New Age Movement: Dancing in the Dark," by Philip H. Lochhaas, in the *Lutheran Witness,* April 1987, page 8. Used by permission of Concordia Publishing House.)

Comedian Johnny Carson and others trivialized the miniseries *Out on a Limb,* to which the above quote refers. Nevertheless, regardless of Shirley MacLaine's involvement, the New Age movement is real! Elsewhere in the article Rev. Lochhaas calls it **"the most anti-God philosophy to come on the scene in recent years, a blatant repetition of Satan's first and most successful temptation: to be as God."**

You may recall from session 26 that the very first part of the creed from *Humanist Manifesto II* claims that placing God above human needs does a disservice to the human species. Couple this with the supposed improvement in the human species suggested by Darwin's theory of evolution, and you find only a small leap needed before humans would put themselves on a level with God. **The New Age movement makes this leap!**

"THEOLOGY" OF THE NEW AGE MOVEMENT

While those within the New Age movement do not spell out a system of beliefs like the Christian creeds, their writings indicate that they believe the following (summarized from the Lochhaas article in the *Lutheran Witness*):

1. **God is not distinct from creation.** God and creation are one, as are matter and energy, good and evil, life and death.

2. **Humanity is one with God: Man is divine.** Humanity, therefore, knows no limits; possibility knows no bounds.

3. **Humanity's crises result from the fact that we are ignorant of our divinity.** One of MacLaine's spirit-guides revealed to her that "there is no such thing as evil. . . . The question is lack of spiritual knowledge, not whether or not there is evil."

4. **Humanity needs transformation** (a New Age buzzword), **with each individual becoming aware of his or her oneness with God.** We are our own creators! As such, we are responsible for everything that happens to us or around us, for there is no reality except as we perceive it. MacLaine said reality "was only what each of us decided it was."

5. **Our perception—and, therefore, reality—can be changed by a myriad of "techniques" that will alter our state of consciousness.** This technique will try to dismantle what we in the past thought was reality. It aims to build a new set of perceptions based on the perceiver being his or her own creator.

New Age techniques can include astrology, hypnosis, chanting, meditation, hyperactivity (such as frenzied dancing), firewalking, prolonged isolation, seances, use of crystals for massage, boot-camp tactics at seminars, or whatever else might produce an altered state of consciousness.

6. Transformation of the individual is the basis for global transformation characterized by mass enlightenment and social unity. Humanity is said to be on the brink of its "final evolutionary leap"—one language, one world government, one monetary system, and maybe even everyone thinking the same thoughts at the same time!

And the time for this is *now.*

REINCARNATION

Belief in karma and reincarnation is an absolute and vital part of the New Age movement.

This philosophy says that only a rare few individuals realize their deity in one lifetime. Usually it take a dozen to thousands of lives for a soul to become enlightened to his or her godhood. We must keep coming back until we "get it right."

Karma—the balance of ignorance and enlightenment—controls each lifetime. Karma is relentless. A person pays and pays until every shred of ignorance is atoned for.

The New Age movement has no concept of forgiveness. Instead, a person pays by failing to achieve godhood in a given existence. This concept can have no "victims"; the sufferings of each lifetime are preordained by the person suffering them. A person might, for example, choose life as a Nazi holocaust victim to burn off bad karma in order to achieve a higher incarnation the next time around.

This concept could deaden a person's attitude toward helping others. Who, after all, would dare to interrupt the law of karma by granting relief to one who has chosen the present state? Our interference would only doom that person to repeat his or her present existence!

APPEAL OF THE NEW AGE MOVEMENT

In the *Lutheran Witness* article Rev. Philip Lochhaas gives four reasons for the New Age attraction:

1. Comfortable and successful people (those most easily attracted) see opportunities for even greater comfort and success.

2. People tend to be proud, and the movement appeals to our "natural religion" of being in total control of our own destiny.

3. The movement assumes that an altered state of consciousness is, of itself, preferable to the normal "unenlightened" state.

4. Satan nimself continues (as he has from the beginning) to make evil appear as good to those who seek to be as God.

RESPONDING TO THE NEW AGE MOVEMENT

This satanic inversion of the truth turns religion into a completely anti-God state of mind. It destroys the relationship between the individual and the Creator by violating the first principle of Scripture regarding human origin. It aims to destroy the uniqueness of Jesus Christ as the Son of God and Savior of the world.

We are at war! Fortunately, we don't need to battle the New Age with new weapons. We need only the "old" weapon we have mentioned so often—**the sword of the Spirit, which is the Word of God (Ephesians 6:17).** Let's look at that Word.

1. What was Satan's oldest temptation **(Genesis 3:5)?**

2. How did God respond when people tried to become like Him in **Genesis 3:16–24?** in **11:7–9?**

3. Describe the aspects of our relationship with God that you find in **Romans 1:17–32.**

4. What do **Ecclesiastes 7:20, Isaiah 64:6;** and **Romans 3:23** tell about our natural condition?

5. What do you learn about being transformed in **Romans 1:16–17? 6:3–4? 8:1–2? 12:1–2? Ephesians 2:4–5?**

6. What do you learn about life after death in **John 14:6? 1 Corinthians 15:42–44, 54–57? 1 Thessalonians 4:13–18?**

REMEMBER

By Him [Jesus] all things were created: things in heaven and on earth, visible and invisible, whether thrones or powers or rulers or authorities; all things were created by Him and for Him. He is before all things, and in Him all things hold together. And He is the Head of the body, the church; He is the Beginning and the Firstborn from among the dead, so that in everything He might have the supremacy. For God was pleased to have all His fullness dwell in Him, and through Him to reconcile to Himself all things, whether things on earth or things in heaven, by making peace through His blood, shed on the cross.

Colossians 1:16–20

Session 40

"But It's Only a Game!"

AS YOU RECEIVED CHRIST, LIVE IN HIM!

Just as you received Christ Jesus as Lord, continue to live in Him, rooted and built up in Him, strengthened in the faith as you were taught, and overflowing with thankfulness. See to it that no one takes you captive through hollow and deceptive philosophy, which depends on human tradition and the basic principles of this world rather than on Christ.
Colossians 2:6– 8

WHAT ABOUT FANTASY?

Fantasy is a part of everyone's life. Some psychologists today express a concern, however, over the types of fantasy encouraged by toys, games, and books that have either mythological (unicorns, dragons, castles) or futuristic (spacemen, robots) characters who operate with supernatural occult powers; by toys that introduce occult practices (magick, spells, sorcery, and incantations) as a part of their life-style; and by videos—including cartoons and movies—that are also dominated by these fantasy characters.

When children choose to play with a toy truck or doll, their imaginations are free to determine the role that toy will have in their play. In a sense, the toy becomes an extension of the child's mind. When, however, children are given a toy that is simultaneously released with a cartoon that describes its behavior, their imagination is limited and is projected in certain directions. This is not always bad, but toys are often predisposed to violence and occult behavior. Toys that suggest violence and occult behavior may pique the child's interest in violence and the occult.

Three incidents from *Turmoil in the Toybox*, by Phil Phillips (Starburst, 1986), illustrate problems that sometimes occur because young children cannot always separate fact from fantasy.

- A Sunday school teacher asked her children to think of ways they could help a younger sister or brother not to be afraid of the dark. One child immediately suggested, "I would tell my little brother that *He-Man* is in the room!"

- A little boy was listening to the radio while riding with his mother in the car one day. A preacher began to pray, "Our Lord God, Master of the Universe . . ." when the little boy jumped up and said, "Mommy, God isn't the master of the universe—*He-Man* is!"

- A mother was sitting at the wheel of her car, sobbing, after she and and her little daughter narrowly avoided an accident. He daughter comforted her with a hand on her shoulder and the words, "Don't worry, Mother. *She-Ra* would have saved us!"

(From *Turmoil in the Toy Box,* by Phil Phillips, published by Starburst Publishers, P.O. box 4123, Lancaster, P.A. 17604; Tel. (717) 569-5558. Used by permission. All rights reserved.)

He-Man and She-Ra were two of the superheroes when Phillips wrote his book. Today the daughter might trust *Thundercat* to save her. Tomorrow will see new superheroes, because the toy manufacturers will develop new cartoons to sell new toys.

1. What happens when a child's hero is a cartoon character (and accompanying toy) that has magical powers or is a mutant—half human and half beast or half human and half robot? or when the character (or the child) can receive superpower by putting on a mask or a shawl? When does "play" cross the brink that separates "fun" from trust in something or someone other than God?

2. Hold a debate about a current cartoon character (if possible, one also sold as a toy). One team should take the position that the character is harmless fun. The other team should take the position that children should not be allowed to watch the cartoon or play with the toy.

DEADLY GAMES AND PLAYING FOR KEEPS!

One well-known *fantasy role-playing* game (FRP) is *Dungeons and Dragons* (D&D). Perhaps the earliest public concern over FRP came when a young undergraduate student at the University of Michigan mysteriously disappeared after several intense sessions of *D&D.* Friends speculated that his disappearance was somehow associated with his intense involvement in *D&D,* and that he had mysteriously disappeared in the

maze of corridors and passages in the game he had been playing!

When he surfaced, unharmed, a month later in Texas, almost everyone agreed that there was no connection between his *D&D* involvement and his disappearance. A year later, when the same young man committed suicide, publicity again sought to make some connection between his death and his *D&D* involvement. A magazine article suggested that TSR Hobbies, Inc., should raise a foundation to him.

Playing with Fire, by John Weldon and James Bjornstad (Moody, 1984), is devoted entirely to the FRP games, such as *D&D*. The authors mention another suicide and a subsequent lawsuit, which cast further shadows on FRP games such as *D&D*. On June 9, 1982, Irving Pulling, 16, came home from school and committed suicide. It was alleged that only a few hours earlier he had been playing *D&D* in school. During the game a "curse was placed on him (on his character) by another player" (p. 19).

Claiming that young people carry over their FRP experiences into real life, his parents believe that this curse disturbed their son and placed him under emotional distress, resulting in his suicide later that day.

The boy's parents claim that, because of the way the game was constructed, their son believed that the only way to remove the curse from himself was to offer a sacrifice. He had calculated that he was 97 percent certain of experiencing a *resurrection* if he was able to sacrifice a human—himself—within a certain time limit!

FRP games like D&D utilize at least seven separate occult practices that are expressly forbidden by Scripture:

1. magick and the casting of spells;
2. protective inscriptions;
3. astral projection or soul travel;
4. necromancy, or communication with the dead;
5. conjuration and summoning of demons and devils;
6. occult alignment with powers or deities;
7. using names of occult or magick orders.

DANGER: OCCULT PRACTICED HERE!

The world of the occult is hidden and secret. Mere contact with these occult practices is often enough to attract people to them. We have no promise that the evil powers of the spirit world won't respond when beckoned in these games! The follow-up, then, would find the player pursuing these occult practices in everyday life.

Clearly, since God expressly forbids occult activities, participation in them displeases Him. So why would we do it? As Scripture warns, Satan prowls about, seeking someone to devour **(1 Peter 5:8).** He can make a game or a toy look desirable and fun. While the excitement might seem attractive, it can also prove to be deadly!

1. Read **2 Corinthian 5:14–15.** What can motivate you to avoid dabbling in occult "games"?

2. Read **Philippians 4:8–9.** What are some true, noble, right, pure, lovely, admirable, excellent, and praiseworthy thoughts or activities that give you more peace and joy than occult activities?

REMEMBER

Whatever is true, whatever is noble, whatever is right, whatever is pure, whatever is lovely, whatever is admirable—if anything is excellent or praiseworthy—think about such things. Whatever you have learned or received or heard from me, or seen in me—put it into practice. And the God of peace will be with you.

Philippians 4:8–9

FOR NEXT TIME

Some popular music has been called into question by parents, educators, and even governmental officials. Find some popular song lyrics that you feel may contain material that is satanic or otherwise displeasing to God.

Session 41

"It's Only a Song!"

PROPERTY OF GOD USE TO HIS GLORY

The earth is the Lord's, and everything in it. . . . So whether you eat or drink or whatever you do, do it all for the glory of God.

1 Corinthians 10:26, 31

MUSIC—BANE OR BLESSING?

1. Saul, the first king of Israel, deserted God, and an evil spirit from the Lord tormented Him. To get relief, Saul asked David to play the harp for him. We read in **1 Samuel 16:23: "Whenever the spirit from God came upon Saul, David would take his harp and play. Then relief would come to Saul; he would feel better, and the evil spirit would leave him."**

2. During a concert in Altamont, CA, in December 1967 a man was clubbed to death with pool cues, fists, and chains, and then stabbed five times as the audience went into a frenzy while Mick Jagger sang "Jumpin' Jack Flash" and "Sympathy for the Devil."

Both incidents involved music, but the results were as different as day and night! What caused the differences?

Obviously, these are extreme examples. But they illustrate the effects music does have. Thousands of times each day people are inspired by music to relax, praise God, meditate, or show kindness. At the same time music moves others to use drugs, abuse sex, rebel against parents, or even commit suicide.

You probably enjoy singing and listening to hymns and other Christian music in church and your school chapel services—at least part of the time. But you might also be saying about now, "Wait a minute! I enjoy other music, too! Don't tell me to throw away all my records and tapes!"

What's a body to do?

MAKING CHOICES

You will need to make some choices. Whether you like rock or country or "Christian rock" or something else, you will find some "very good" music and some "very bad" music. As you decide which music you will listen to, consider these five criteria:

1. **Lyrics.** What kinds of lyrics are acceptable and what makes others objectionable? Share some example of "good" and "bad" lyrics in music you know.

2. **Names of performing groups.** Some groups choose names with negative connotations—perhaps related to sex or drugs or Satan and the occult. Can you give some examples? If the name gives a negative impression, what would you expect of the music?

3. **Album names and covers.** Judge names in the same way you judge names of groups. Visuals may show nudity, perverted sex, drugs, or demonic figures and signs. What examples can you give?

4. **Public performances.** Contrast a "Christian" rock performance with one that includes mimicking sexual acts on stage, destruction of equipment, nudity, transvestism, or mutilation of animals.

5. **Personal lives of the performers.** This, of course, may not directly affect the music being performed. Talk, though, about the impact of a "star" who blatantly abuses alcohol, other drugs, or sex, or who challenges the authority of parents, or who debunks religion or praises satanism.

RATE YOUR MUSIC AND PERFORMERS

As a class, rate 10 popular songs. Use the following steps:

1. Agree on the 10 songs you will rate.

2. Discuss the lyrics of the first song. (If possible, ask someone to read them aloud.)

3. *Individually,* rate the lyrics on a scale of 1 (very bad) to 10 (excellent).

4. Discuss other aspects of the same song (quality of the song, performer, album, etc.).

5. *Individually,* assign one rating (between 1 and 10) for those aspects of the song.

6. Follow steps 2 to 5 for the other songs.

7. Tabulate your votes for the lyrics, and find an average for each song.

8. Tabulate your votes for the other aspects, and find an average for each song.

If you wish, also rate some albums or performing groups.

Now talk about your findings. How will they affect your listening habits? Do you think you should share your findings with others? If so, with whom? How can you share them?

Also talk about songs you did not rate today—songs you know and songs not yet in existence. How will you decide whether to listen to them? Can others in your class help you? Can other friends? Would you like the help of teachers? your parents? other adults? **Plan a strategy to help you become a *discriminating* listener.**

PARENTS, MUSIC, AND YOU

Has your mother or father ever told you, "Turn off the stereo!" or "Turn that music down"? Music becomes a major area of contention in many homes. Usually that happens when parents do not like the kind of music their teenagers listen to or do not like how loud they play the music.

God desires happy families, not families that bicker over music. Talk about things *you* can do to get rid of this kind of barrier to communication in your home. Do you think your parents would be willing to sit down with you and rate music as you did in the previous section? Do you think they would also be willing to rate music *they* listen to—perhaps country music? Develop several strategies to help you overcome this barrier to parent-teen relationships. Then pick one for you to use at home.

MUSIC: GOD'S GIFT OR SATAN'S TOOL?

Music truly is a gift from God. But like God's other beautiful gifts—such as money, sexuality, and authority—Satan finds a weakness and exploits it. Scripture often refers to the use of music and musical instruments to praise God **(Psalm 149:1; 150:3–5)**, but we also find that music has been used in the worship of Satan and his influences **(Exodus 32:17–18; Daniel 3:4–6)**.

Satan, as the father of lies **(John 8:44)**, likes nothing better than to discredit, blaspheme, and mock God **(Revelation 13:1, 6–7)**. God, however, tells us who have been bought with the price of the blood of Jesus to honor Him with our lives **(1 Corinthians 6:18–20)**. Even though we live in the world, we are not to be of the world **(John 17:14)**. And we have God's assurance that, despite all the temptations we face, He will keep us in the faith that He gave us **(Philippians 1:6)**.

In all things, including our purchase and use of music, we may be required to be different or separate from the rest of the world **(2 Corinthians 6:14–18)**. Even though a great number of people see nothing wrong with the ungodly living encouraged by certain popular music, we must stand firm with the truth of Jesus Christ. In His Word He tells us the truth about how He wants us to live **(John 17:17)**.

That's not always easy! As a matter of fact, it's impossible when we rely on our own power. Thanks be to God, we have His power at our disposal! To review how God makes you alive in Him, read **Ephesians 2:1–10**. Maybe you can read this together as a closing devotion for this session.

REMEMBER

You, dear children, are from God and have overcome them, because the One who is in you is greater than the one who is in the world. They are from the world and therefore speak from the viewpoint of the world, and the world listens to them. We are from God, and whoever knows God listens to us; but whoever is not from God does not listen to us. This is how we recognize the Spirit of truth and the spirit of falsehood.

1 John 4:4–6

Session 42

Review of Sessions 34–41

Give brief, yet complete, answers to the following questions.

1. Define the word *occult.*

2. How do you know that the explosive increase in satanic activity is a sign of the approaching end of the world?

3. Show that you understand that we are engaged in a *war* with Satan, by giving examples of some of the military terminology used in Scripture.

4. Briefly recall several incorrect attitudes toward satanism; then outline a proper, Scriptural attitude.

5. Describe the extremely dangerous aspects of Satan noted in **Ephesians 6:11–18** and **1 Peter 5:8–9.**

6. Define the word *astrology,* giving its derivation.

7. Tell how astrology probably came into being.

8. Show how God's Word condemns astrology and its purposes.

9. List several of the dangers of being involved in astrology.

10. Aside from the difference in spelling, describe the differences between illusionary magic and occult magick.

11. Give Scriptural examples to show that God opposes those who practice magick.

12. How do you know that you should turn to God when you seek power and wisdom?

13. By citing an example of how Jesus dealt with Satan, show that you have the same resources at your disposal.

14. Define the term *spiritism.*

15. From **1 Samuel 28** and **1 Chronicles 10,** show that God forbids and condemns *all* spiritistic practices.

16. Tell why God is so strongly opposed to any attempts to contact the dead.

17. Tell how the experiences of Bishop James Pike demonstrate that even a strong Christian can be fooled by Satan.

18. Show how satanism can be so highly organized, and yet relatively invisible.

19. Briefly describe Anton LaVey and Mike Warnke's involvement in satanism.

20. Show several of the *hooks* Satan uses to catch people in his evil web.

21. From **Romans 1** demonstrate that satanism is another form of idolatry.

22. Which words from **Matthew 4** give comfort to us in our battle against Satan?

23. Describe the New Age movement.

24. Demonstrate the the New Age movement contradicts Scripture.

25. List and briefly describe six major themes usually present in New Age thinking.

26. Why must we exercise care in the purchase and use of toys?

27. Suggest several guidelines that you, if you were now a parent, would use in buying toys and games for your children.

28. What are the basic Scriptural objections to *Dungeons and Dragons?*

29. What does **1 Corinthians 10:26, 31** have to say about our use of music?

30. If you were a musician, what goals would you choose for your music?

31. What are some criteria you will use to determine which tapes and records to buy?

UNIT 7

Your Faith and Others

Since you attend a Lutheran high school, do you live in a protected environment? Some critics say so. They also suggest that once you leave this protected environment, you will be unable to handle the challenges of the "real" world. These critics assume that students who attend parochial schools cannot get along with people who have other beliefs.

Do you agree? How do you look at religions other than your own? Can you respect other beliefs?Have you ever considered that all other religions are simply human attempts at answering the most important of life's questions?

In this final unit we will tackle some of these questions. We will examine how we can remain sensitive to others' faith.

How do you respect the sincerity of their beliefs, while remaining true to your own belief in Jesus as *the only way to heaven?* It's not easy.

We are warned to be firm in our faith, not wavering like a wave of the sea (**James 1:6).** Notice how Paul describes this growth in **Ephesians 4:14–16: "Then we will no longer be infants, tossed back and forth by the waves, and blown here and there by every wind of teaching and by the cunning and craftiness of men in their deceitful scheming. Instead, speaking the truth in love, we will in all things grow up into Him who is the Head, that is, Christ. From Him the whole body, joined and held together by every supporting ligament, grows and builds itself up in love, as each part does its work."**

Spiritual maturity involves respect for those who are different. But it's more. Even as we respect the faith of others, we also make a firm, clear witness to our faith in Jesus Christ as the only Savior of the world.

May our Savior fill you with patience as you wait for opportunities to share your faith, and may He give you the courage to do so boldly when asked. Peace in Jesus!

Session 43

Relating to the Faith of Others

WE DON'T LIVE IN A VACUUM

Do you remember the incident recorded in Acts 10? Peter, a Jewish Christian and apostle of the Lord, had been out preaching about Jesus Christ. He was staying at a home in Joppa.

The Lord had directed a Gentile, Cornelius, to invite Peter to come to Caesarea to preach Jesus to the people there. As Cornelius' servants were on their way, the Lord also spoke to Peter. As a Jew, Peter had made distinctions between clean and unclean. Now Peter distinctly heard the Lord say to him, **"Do not call anything impure that God has made clean" (10:15).** When Cornelius' servants arrived, Peter went down, greeted these people, and invited them into the house. The next day he set off for Caesarea with them.

When he began to talk to Cornelius, along with his family and friends, Peter related to them why God had arranged for him to come to them: **"I now realize how true it is that God does not show favoritism but accepts men from every nation who fear Him and do what is right" (10:34–35).** God had shown Peter that he dare not allow his own mistaken beliefs regarding food, etc., make him biased toward others. Peter proceeded to share the message of Jesus Christ with them and baptize them.

1. *How* do you think God wants us to relate to people of other faiths? Do you think he wants us to ignore them? Should we invite them into our homes? Would we be wrong if we spent some time with them, learning their customs and beliefs, and then told them about our faith in Jesus? To what extent could we join them for the purpose of witnessing to them about our faith in Jesus as the only Savior from sin? *Talk about it.*

Also recall an episode from **Acts 17:14–33.** The apostle Paul had traveled to Athens. While he was awaiting the arrival of Silas and Timothy, who had stayed behind in Berea, Paul toured the city. He noticed many religious idols and became involved in a religious dispute with some philosophers. They invited him into their meeting at a famous place called the Areopagus, or Mars Hill. They knew his was a new teaching. They asked him about it. What an opportunity!

(What would you say? Would you be frightened? Remember, they outnumbered him considerably. And Paul was on their turf!)

Paul didn't back down one bit. He started with something they were familiar with: **"Men of Athens! I see that in every way you are very religious! For as I walked around and looked carefully at your objects of worship, I even found an altar with this inscription: 'to an unknown God.' Now what you worship as something unknown, I am going to proclaim to you" (17:22–23).**

From his sightseeing, Paul probably didn't know a whole lot about these people and their beliefs. But he did know that they were religious. He also was alert to the fact that they were somewhat uncertain about their worship. Just in case they didn't have all the bases covered, they had included one altar to the "unknown God." Paul seized this opportunity! Although his success wasn't great in numbers, he did manage to convert some members of the council that met there on Mars Hill. They became followers of Jesus that very day! What a neat story!

Without agreeing with them, Paul used something from their religion to witness to his faith in Jesus Christ. He seized the situation at hand and shared Jesus with the people the Lord provided.

2. We don't live in a vacuum. Daily we interact with other people. Now, how do you respond to their faith? Do you put them down? Or do you simply ignore their beliefs? Have you ever worked with someone and not known what religion they were? Do you think others around you know what church you attend, and *in whom* you are trusting for eternal life? Where do you get the power and boldness to talk about your faith **(Ephesians 2:5, 10; 2 Corinthians 5:14, 17–20)?** *Talk about it.*

IT'S NEVER TOO LATE TO LEARN

Even though you disagree with the beliefs of certain people, might you be able to learn something from them? Do you admire something about them? Does the behavior of some people suggest ways you can improve your own religious practices or how you can better express your faith in God?

Consider those Jehovah's Witnesses who spend up to 40 hours a month going door to door talking to people about what they believe. How can God use *you* to witness to strangers?

How about young Mormons who must commit two years of their lives to being missionaries? At their own expense they go door to door with the message of Mormonism. Could you do more missionary work around you, or perhaps go somewhere else with the message of the Savior?

What about the Hindus or Buddhists? Consider their dignified self-discipline! Of course, they believe they can somehow appease God by denying their flesh. You can deny your flesh because Jesus, who was crucified for you, empowers you to crucify your own flesh **(Galatians 5:24).**

What about your own prayer life? God encourages us to pray continually **(1 Thessalonians 5:17).** Consider the Muslim, who bows toward the east five times a day and prays to Allah. How do things stand with *your* prayer life?

Perhaps certain religious groups lead you to think of other exemplary practices. Perhaps you begin to feel guilty. As this happens, remember a couple things: All those "good" actions count nothing toward earning salvation **(Galatians 3:10–11),** and God's love for us does not depend upon our "goodness" **(Romans 5:8–10).**

Empowered by your faith in Jesus and His presences in your life, you can grow in greater love of God and devotion to the kind of life He wants for you. God promises: **"Just as you received Christ Jesus as Lord, continue to live in Him, rooted and built up in Him, strengthened in the faith as you were taught, and overflowing with thankfulness" (Colossians 2:6).** We don't earn God's favor by our behavior. We can't! We can only thank Him that for Christ's sake we are already *in* His favor, forever! And because of Him, we can live like it.

BE AWARE OF DANGEROUS BELIEFS

As you relate to other faiths, **be aware that the beliefs of some groups may be dangerous to your faith.** What are some of those groups? What are their dangerous beliefs?

Consider cults that use deceptive recruiting practices. Or groups that prey on sinful tendencies—like sexual desires or satisfying God with our works. Think about the humanistic tendency to place humanity, rather than God, at the center of religion, and about the New Age movement, which actually teaches that we are gods!

We dare not compromise our Christian faith. Christianity is a *unique* religion. As God says, **"Salvation is found in no one else, for there is no other name under heaven ... by which we must be saved" (Acts 4:12).** Jesus didn't encourage us to ignore differences in beliefs. He said, **"I am the Way and the Truth and the Life. No one comes to the Father except through Me" (John 14:6).**

SHARE HOPE, AND NOT HOSTILITY

Perhaps you've had Jehovah's Witnesses persist in arguing with you at your door, and you've wanted to slam the door in their face. Please don't! You may feel frustrated, but consider the words of Peter: **"Always be prepared to give an answer to everyone who asks you to give the reason for the hope that you have, but do this with gentleness and respect" (1 Peter 3:15).**

Notice two important things in that statement. Share your *hope,* and do it with *gentleness.* How do those two words describe how you should relate to people of other faiths? Do you share your *hope,* or do you argue about some point of doctrine? Are you *gentle,* or do you become rather argumentative? Consider which would make the best witness for Jesus. *Talk about it.*

As you witness, be sure to share your own sincerity of faith. Then invite them to join with you in a celebration of the close relationship you have with Jesus Christ—eternally!

REMEMBER

We are therefore Christ's ambassadors, as though God were making His appeal through us. We implore you on Christ's behalf: be reconciled to God.
2 Corinthians 5:20

FOR NEXT TIME

How could you most clearly witness your faith in Jesus to a cult a member? Be specific.

Session 44

Replacing Fear with Confidence

He died for all, that those who live should no longer live for themselves but for Him who died for them and was raised again.

2 Corinthians 5:15

FEARS

Do you know someone who is afraid of the dark, perhaps a little brother or sister? Why are they afraid of the dark? Perhaps they are afraid of the bogeyman. Do you think sometimes grown people are afraid of something they can't really see?

We may fear things that aren't even there. But we may also fear things that are very real. For example, some people are afraid of flying in an airplane, for fear of crashing. Others are afraid of snakes. While there really is something to fear in these cases, those people probably have never crashed in an airplane or been bitten by a snake.

Some people are afraid of themselves and of the things they have done wrong. It has been said that all people have "a skeleton in their closet." Do you have "a skeleton in your closet"? You probably don't want to tell others what it is that you are ashamed of, but have you ever lived in fear that someone would find out? Did you ever wonder what would happen if someone did find out and would tell others your deepest, darkest secrets? Would you be embarrassed? Why? How do you feel, knowing that God is aware of *all* your secrets?

What are you afraid of? Since everyone has sinned, everyone at one time or another probably feels a fear of dying and going to hell. Are you afraid of going to hell? Why or why not?

Because you believe in Jesus, that fear isn't real for you right now. But others are afraid of hell right now. And in their own way, they are trying very hard to do something to avoid hell. That's where you come in. You can share with them that there is really nothing that *they* need to do to earn heaven—nor anything they *can* do. It is a free gift!

Perhaps you have another fear. Have you ever wondered how you would witness to someone of another religion? What if that person knows more than you? Or can out-argue you? Would you be afraid? feel inadequate?

That's where Jesus comes in. He predicted that we would be placed into situations in which we would be asked to witness to others. He even hinted that we might be asked to share our faith with people in high places **(Matthew 10:17–18).** But He also promised us that we wouldn't be alone. He said, **"When they arrest you, do not worry about what to say or how to say it. At that time you will be given what to say, for it will not be you speaking, but the Spirit of your Father speaking through you" (10:19–20).**

If you are afraid of being inadequate to witness to people of other religions, relax. You won't be alone. Think of the words of the hymn: "If you cannot speak like angels, If you cannot preach like Paul, You can tell the love of Jesus; You can say he died for all" (*Lutheran Worship* 318, stanza 2). His perfect love casts out all fear!

CONFIDENCE

Is there anything in the whole world that you trust completely? Do you trust your best friend? Do you trust your parents? your brothers and sisters? Do you have a *special someone* you could trust when everyone else is failing you?

Think, for example, about standing on the top of a very tall ladder. Whom would you want to be holding the bottom? Would you trust the strongest person you know? Or someone who is very careful?

Did you ever consider that when it comes to your

eternal life, you can't trust the strongest or the smartest or the most careful person you know? Instead, you have to trust in Jesus.

Way back in the first sessions we said that there were really only two religions in the world. There is the religion of God, in which people trust in Jesus alone to save them. And there is the religion of people, in which people trust in themselves and what they have done to save themselves.

A lot of people in this world are trusting in themselves and, if they could be perfectly honest, they feel pretty shaky! They are trusting in their own works to get them closer to God. But that won't work. Not only will it not get them any closer to God, they can't really gain any comfort from it, either. That's because they can never know when they've done enough!

A man owed so much money to the bank that he thought he could never pay off the loan. So late one night he left town, and didn't tell anyone where he was going. After he had gone, his friends realized why he had run away, and they took up a collection and paid off his loan at the bank. The man spent many miserable years in a faraway city, scrimping and saving. He went without many things, but finally he saved enough money to repay the bank. He returned to the town, went straight to the bank and announced to the president of the bank why he had come.

The surprised bank president showed the even more surprised man that there was no balance due on the account book. His friends had repaid the loan in full. The surprised man couldn't believe it. All those years he had "gone without," and he didn't owe anything!

So many religions are like that. People are working furiously so that they can get some comfort, and they never do! They scrimp and they save. They "go without." And for what? They don't have any comfort.

We know that God "went without" for us. He "went without" His only Son. He paid our debts—those we could never repay. And when we return to His "bank," He shows us that there is no amount due on the account books. We have been set free by the blood of Jesus Christ.

In the story, the man was sad that he hadn't checked the account books earlier. God calls us to help other people see that the "account books" of sin have been cleared forever.

We have confidence, not because of anything we have done, but because of what Christ has already done for us **(Romans 5:1)**. We can be free from the burden, guilt, and punishment of sin, because they aren't there anymore. By dying on the cross, Christ took them away **(John 3:16)**! By faith in Christ we are free **(John 8:32)**—free from our sin and free (and empowered!) to share the confidence God gives us.

We can share this confidence with those who don't yet know Jesus. And with those who know *about* Jesus but haven't yet come into a living relationship with Him and don't have the same confidence that you have. Don't worry about what you will say. The Holy Spirit will be with you. He will give you the right words to say. Just speak about Jesus. Tell them what He has done for you.

And may God bless you!

SUGGESTIONS FOR WITNESSING TO NON-CHRISTIANS

1. Invite them to be God's friends, too **(2 Corinthians 5:20)**. Don't be hostile! Share with them a simple Bible passage, like **John 3:16.** You may wish to put their name into the verse to personalize it for them.

2. Sometimes you have to get away from people—shake the dust off your feet against them **(Matthew 10:14)**. But remember that if you can't witness to this particular person, maybe someone else can. Don't close the door for someone else! Try to depart on a friendly basis!

3. Talk with them. Often they will want to do all the talking. At the very beginning, agree that you each will have a certain amount of time to talk. Stick to your agreement. No one was won through a heated argument. You can't convert someone yourself. Simply share the Word of God with them. Remember that it is the Holy Spirit who does the converting **(1 Corinthians 12:3).**

4. Be calm. Remember that you have Jesus on your side. You have no reason to be afraid **(Matthew 10:19–20)**. Share the simple message of Law and Gospel, and wait for the Holy Spirit to do the rest!

REMEMBER

Always be prepared to give an answer to everyone who asks you to give the reason for the hope that you have. But do this with gentleness and respect.
1 Peter 3:15

Remember to share your *hope,* and to do so *gently* and *respectfully!*

Session 45

Review of Sessions 1–44

Give brief, yet complete, answers to the following questions.

1. How would you respond to someone who said, "All religions are the same. All that is important is that you are sincere in what you believe"?

2. Explain what we mean when we say that there are only two religions in the world.

3. What is the difference between "religion" and "faith"?

4. Buddhism and Hinduism both share a common belief in Nirvana. Explain.

5. Buddhism and Hinduism differ in their concept of a supreme being. Explain.

6. In what ways does Islam differ vastly from Christianity, and it what ways is it similar?

7. Name prophets who are accepted by Judaism, Islam, and Christianity.

8. List three Bible verses you could use in sharing your Christian faith with someone who belonged to one of the major world religions, and demonstrate that you understand how you would use each one.

9. How does a Buddhist's motivation for denying oneself differ from a Christian's motivation?

10. Define "catholic" and "orthodox."

11. Describe the circumstances preceding the event which, in 1054, divided the Eastern and Western churches.

12. Describe the circumstances preceding the event which, in 1517, began a major split between the protesting Christians and the Roman Catholic Church.

13. Explain the contributions the following people made to the development of Christianity: Wycliffe, Hus, Luther, Zwingli, Calvin, and Wesley.

14. Explain the governmental issues that distracted the Holy Roman emperor at the time of Luther's protest and which perhaps contributed to the rapid and solid development of the Lutheran Reformation.

15. Explain the importance of the phrase, "salvation by grace, through faith in Jesus Christ," for Lutheran theology.

16. Explain three ways Christians have sought to overcome the separation of church groups into denominations.

17. Describe Calvinism.

18. Describe Arminianism.

19. Describe synergism.

20. Explain a possible danger each of the above three poses for historic Christianity.

21. Using **2 Timothy 4:3–4,** explain the rapid rise of cults in our country. Include things about our country and about people in general that stimulate cultic growth.

22. Describe several characteristics that would alert you that a particular group is a cult.

23. What does the Bible mean when it says to **test the spirits (1 John 4:1)?**

24. Explain some deceptive recruiting techniques used by cults.

25. Name and describe a cult that attacks the Trinity and especially the deity of Jesus Christ.

26. Name and describe a cult that features "new" revelation, added to the Bible, as the source of authority.

27. What unique claim does the Worldwide Church of God make concerning its ancestry?

28. In what way does **Deuteronomy 18:22** help us determine that Armstrong, for example, was not a true prophet of God?

29. What beliefs of Adventism are dangerous to Christian beliefs? Why?

30. Explain how humanism has attacked the authority of Christian beliefs in our country.

31. How does **Proverbs 14:12** describe humanism and, in fact, many other cults?

32. In what ways do cults require new recruits to make *sacrifices* in order to join?

33. Briefly describe how Rev. Moon's teachings *begin* with the Bible, but rapidly conflict with it.

34. Describe several practices of Hare Krishna.

35. What occult-based technique did Mary Baker Eddy learn from Phineas P. Quimby? How did she use this technique to found the Church of Christ, Scientist?

36. What techniques are used to control minds?

37. Explain both sides of the brainwashing controversy.

38. Using three Bible passages, describe how you would witness to a member of a particular cult. (Name which group you are working with!)

39. Define the word *occult.*

40. Why has occult activity been rapidly increasing recently?

41. Describe several incorrect attitudes toward the occult. Then briefly state a correct, Biblical position toward the occult.

42. Describe astrology, witchcraft, magick, and spiritism.

43. Use several Bible passages to demonstrate that God absolutely condemns all occult activity.

44. Cite incidents from the life of a famous American church worker to describe the dangers of becoming involved in spiritism.

45. From **Matthew 4,** show that we too can successfully stand against Satan.

46. Describe the New Age movement and the dangerous results of the infiltration of New Age thinking in many areas.

47. Explain the dangers of using games like *Dungeons and Dragons*.

48. Explain how certain toys could be dangerous to Christian faith.

49. In what ways can rock music be hazardous to Christian faith?

50. How best can you be aware and sensitive to the religious beliefs of others while you seek to share your faith in Jesus with them?

www.ingramcontent.com/pod-product-compliance
Lightning Source LLC
Chambersburg PA
CBHW062050090426
42740CB00016B/3084